SURREAL:

HOW REALITY TV AND INFLUENCERS CHANGE OUR PERCEPTION OF THE WORLD

D1596276

CLARE CARLUCCIO

NEW DEGREE PRESS

SURREAL: HOW REALITY TV AND INFLUENCERS
CHANGE OUR PERCEPTION OF THE WORLD

ISBN   978-1-64137-922-9   *Paperback*

978-1-64137-699-0   *Kindle Ebook*

978-1-64137-701-0   *Ebook*

SURREAL: HOW REALITY TV AND INFLUENCERS CHANGE OUR PERCEPTION OF THE WORLD

To my wonderful family, which has absolutely nothing in common with the families you can watch on E!

CONTENTS

"Fame can be addictive."

– KIM KARDASHIAN

SURREAL TIMES

———

"Kim Kardashian Meeting Donald Trump in the Oval Office Is a Nightmare We Can't Wake Up From."[1]

This headline in the *New Yorker* perfectly articulates—albeit dramatically—the twilight zone reality we are living in. The infamous gathering, which took place in May of 2018, was, shockingly, a private meeting between the President of the United States and a reality star. Well, that sentence isn't fully accurate, as the President of the United States in question is also a reality star. Puzzling times.

Kim Kardashian arrived in the West Wing without a film camera, her famous family, or her team. She was dressed modestly, but far more fashionably than most, and it was clear that she arrived in D.C. to fulfill a mission.

"I was very focused," Kardashian stated of her time in D.C. "I knew that if I have this meeting, I can't go in there and talk

———

1   Fry, "Kim Kardashian Donald Trump Nightmare," May 31, 2018.

about all the policies that I don't agree with . . . I had to make the decision that this was bigger than me." [2]

Kardashian scheduled the meeting with President Trump to discuss the legal challenges of a woman named Alice Marie Johnson. Kardashian first learned of Johnson's situation after watching a video that was published on the online news site *Mic* profiling Johnson's prison sentence and the infractions that led to a life locked up.

Johnson, now a sixty-three-year-old grandmother, was imprisoned in 1996 and received a life sentence for a first-time, non-violent drug offense. Johnson's story stuck with Kardashian. While she didn't have any direct ties to Johnson, nor had she been directly impacted by similar troubles, Kardashian is a celebrity who has made her share of public mistakes and has, time and again, found her way out of the muck and back to her throne of stardom.

She identified with Johnson's situation and sought to help.

Kardashian reached out to her socialite peer, Ivanka Trump, the President's daughter. Ivanka Trump's husband, Jared Kushner, was leading President Trump's task force to address prison reform. The conversations, which occurred over months prior to the Trump-Kardashian summit in the Oval Office, focused on the details of Johnson's case and the institutional legal issues that led a first time offending single mother to be saddled with a life sentence.

---

2   Hardwood, "Kim Kardashian says Trump 'Compassionate'," June 8, 2018.

In an interview Kardashian gave in the month prior to her visit, she shared that she would "explain to [Trump] that, just like everybody else, we can make choices in our lives that we're not proud of and that we don't think through all the way."[3]

Fast forward a month and the summit of reality TV's First Families officially arrived, but with surprisingly little social media fanfare from Kardashian herself.

Let's pause for a second. If you are human being who has watched TV, or even walked past a magazine stand in the past decade, you've heard of Kim Kardashian. If you are at all like me, you know a lot about Kim, but if you don't, I won't judge you. You are missing out on a major cultural phenomenon and some truly captivating television, for which I feel sorry for you, but I won't judge. Instead, I'll share a little bit of what you're missing out on.

Kim Kardashian is no stranger to sharing the most intimate details of her life with the general public. As the centerpiece of the Kardashian family's reality TV empire, Kim has spent much of her life in the spotlight. She provides a wide-open window into her life in Calabasas, the squabbles she has with her sisters, and the demanding schedule of events, fashion shoots, and promotional engagements she keeps to manage her many product empires.

And, when the TV cameras aren't rolling, Kardashian is sharing selfies (well, pictures of herself, not exactly the selfies we

---

3   Fox, "Keeping up with the Kushners," May 30, 2018.

all try and take with an outstretched arm holding up a cell-phone; hers appear to be professionally-staged photo shoots) when dressed for a night out in full couture and "glam" hair and makeup, or wearing next to nothing at all showing off her famous figure. The woman has taken so many selfies, she actually published a book—*Selfish*—compiling her social media imagery in print for purchase and display on your own coffee table.

So, that's why it's notable that during the meeting to discuss Alice Marie Johnson's prison sentence, Kim seemingly shifted the attention off of herself.

Kardashian made her case to the President and, upon leaving the meeting, noted that Trump was "compassionate" and "sympathetic" to Johnson's situation.[4] Her social media amplifications similarly focused on the woman whose cause she had taken up. She shared an Instagram story of the Presidential seal, with a simple note to Alice Marie Johnson wishing her a happy birthday and reiterating that the focus of the day was all about her case and sentencing.[5]

Kardashian additionally shared two straightforward messages on Twitter, both thanking the President for the opportunity to make her case. She stated that she was hopeful that Trump would grant Johnson clemency and reiterated that she hoped Johnson—and others in similar challenging legal battles—will get a second chance in life.

---

4   Fox, "Keeping up with the Kushners," May 30, 2018.
5   Kim Kardashian, Instagram photo, May 30, 2018.

But, despite Kardashian's reserved publicity strategy for her meeting with President Trump, media attention—both traditional and social—spiraled into a frenzy following the meeting. Much of the attention pointed to a tweet from President Trump himself, which featured a photo of the two set behind the iconic desk of the Oval Office, between an American flag and the flag of the Presidential seal.[6]

Memes circulated social media celebrating the long-awaited Trump-Kim summit, a tongue-in-cheek reference to the hotly anticipated summit—then still in planning—between the President and the leader of North Korea, Kim Jung Un. The *New York Daily News* headlined that she was "The Only Kim He Could Get."[7]

"The Other Big Ass Summit: Trump meets Rump" was the front page headline in the *New York Post* whose article noted that "Kim Thong Un pitch[ed] prez on prison reform."[8] (Though it is worth noting that the *Post* received a fair amount of backlash from these overly sexualized jokes made at Kardashian's expense, which suggests that perhaps there is hope for society, yet.)

Democratic pundit, Daniel Pfeiffer, joked on Twitter that it was a "photo of a reality TV star with no discernible talent, but famous for being famous and a Kardashian."[9]

---

6   Donald Trump, Twitter pose, May 30, 2018.
7   New York Daily News, Twitter post, May 30, 2018.
8   Front Page, The New York Post. May 31, 2018.
9   Dan Pfeiffer, Twitter Post, May 30, 2018.

Audiences questioned Kardashian's credibility as an advocate for prison reform—Kardashian has seemingly led a
charmed life and has not had many interactions with the
American justice system. Some even joked that the most
exposure Kim has had to prison sentencing policies was an
incident filmed in an early season of *Keeping Up With the
Kardashians* when her mother, Kris Jenner, reprimanded
Kim for taking selfies in the car as the family drove her
sister Khloe to prison.[10]

You see, during the 2008 season of *Keeping Up With the
Kardashians*, it is revealed that Khloe violated the terms
of her parole following a DUI she received in 2007. Khloe
didn't report for the road cleanup community service she
was required to complete as part of her sentence. So, a judge
ordered Khloe to thirty days in prison as a result. She was
released three hours after arriving, with the prison citing
overcrowding as the rationale for her very early release.

But before learning how short Khloe's stint in lockup would
be, Kris, Kim and Khloe show little concern for the fact that
Khloe is about to go to jail—as if they knew she wouldn't
truly be held. On the drive out to the prison, Kris suggests
that they stop for breakfast at IHOP if they arrive early for
Khloe's self-surrender. The Kardashian's often-overlooked
brother, Rob, calls Khloe and doesn't even realize that she is
heading to prison or that he should have said goodbye. And
the entire time, Kim has a point-and-shoot camera out and
is snapping photos of herself, her mother, and her sisters—
completely made-up for their big prison arrival. Kris finally

---

10   *Keeping up With the Kardashians*. Season 3, Episode 1. "Free Khloe."

snaps at Kim stating, "Kim, would you stop taking pictures of yourself, your sister is going to JAIL."[11]

Kim later released the photos that she took during that car ride on her personal blog because in her words, she "had to share them with you guys because they are SO funny and I still can't believe this happened."[12]

Given this nonchalance at the idea of her sibling spending a month in prison, you can understand why some were skeptical of Kim's credibility as a voice for prison reform.

But, as it turns out, real action resulted from her meeting with President Trump.

Kardashian was right to note in interviews following the May meeting that he had seemed sympathetic to Johnson's struggles, because, on June 6, 2018, President Trump granted Alice Marie Johnson a full Presidential pardon.

Now, a majorly influential celebrity using her platform to advocate for the wellbeing of another woman in a challenging situation is a positive development in the influence economy. Especially when that woman has served due time for a drug charge that disproportionately incarcerates Black Americans and frequently saddles first-time offenders (like Johnson) with major sentences. Kardashian's adoption of Alice Marie Johnson's case raised awareness for the inequalities and racial bias in American drug offense sentencing policies.

---

11   Ibid.

12   Bueno, "Kim Kardashian Shares Pics of Khloe Going to Jail," March 10, 2016

And, ultimately, her attention to this cause gave Alice Marie Johnson time back with her family—time she never thought she would get to share with loved ones.

But, in considering this extreme situation, I can only question how we got to the point where one person's social media reach could result in a White House meeting and full Presidential pardon. How did we get here?

THE RISE OF THE 'FAMOUS FOR BEING FAMOUS'

There was a time when we only cared about famous people because of their talents. Their exceptional abilities to perform—musically, athletically, dramatically—gave us a reason to sit up and pay attention to them. Our interest in the rich and famous, of course, extended beyond their talents, to a degree. Just like with our personal friends, no one relationship between fan and the famous is entirely defined by a single attribute. We would look at the crowds that the rich and famous associate with, examine their beauty regimens, take their advice on the products and lifestyle hacks they use to maintain health and wellness—but at the end of the day these celebrities were stars because of their talents.

It's not an exclusively modern phenomenon either. F. Scott Fitzgerald leveraged his literary works to launch himself and his wife Zelda into the spotlight throughout the jazz age. There isn't a single American child who hasn't heard the legendary baseball accomplishments of Babe Ruth or Jackie Robinson. And there are oceans of actors, actresses, and TV personalities who have become household names throughout their careers: Tom Cruise, Brad Pitt, Denzel Washington, Meryl Streep, Halle Berry, and on and on.

Today, however, many of our most admired don't need the profession.

The Kardashian pop-cultural phenomenon encapsulates everything we think of when we hear the term *celebrity*: wealth, excess, access, beauty, and scandal. They are linked to famous musicians, rappers, athletes, and icons. They can directly engage millions of fans worldwide with the tap of a button.

But what are their talents?

Their fame is wholly divorced from their contributions to society and industry. Their celebrity is instead linked to the idea of being famous for being famous. Consider Kim. She took a friendship with a socialite (Paris Hilton) added a sex tape scandal and created an empire.

Kim and her sisters—with the strong guidance of momager Kris Jenner—altered the nature of celebrity and influence at its core through their reality TV show, *Keeping Up With the Kardashians*, which debuted in 2007. The show also debuted a brilliant direct-to fan engagement strategy.

See, *Keeping Up With the Kardashians*, built on a foundation established by a number of other reality television programs, including *An American Family* the 1973 television documentary on PBS that followed the activities of the Loud Family, an upper-middle class family in Santa Barbara, California. This program is largely regarded as the very first reality television program, and was intended to chronicle the daily life of the Louds, but quickly revealed what we all really want to see anyway—drama.

The program ultimately documented the break-up of the Loud family, including a daily chronicle of Lance Loud, one of the children, an openly gay man living in New York—a shocking revelation at the time. It showcased a number of tense conversations about Lance's "lifestyle" between Lance and his parents. But, most notably, the show chronicled Bill Loud's extramarital affairs and frequent business trips that lead his wife, Pat Loud, to lament the state of their relationship, discuss his infidelity with her family, and ultimately to file for divorce and kick Bill out of their house. All, of course, captured for the viewing pleasure of the general public.

The Louds laid the foundation for more recent reality TV experiences like *The Osbournes*, focused on musician Ozzy Osborne and his family and *The Simple Life*, which followed socialites Paris Hilton and Nicole Richie as they tried their hands at hard labor around the country. These shows "one upped each other's outrageousness," but ultimately fizzled out over time.[13]

However, with *Keeping Up With the Kardashians*—currently airing its eighteenth season—the family has capitalized on the public desire into the daily lives of the wealthy and privileged, and turned their platform into a long-term money-making enterprise.

---

13   Yardley, "Bill Loud Dead at 97," July 27, 2018.

Over the past two decades, the Kardashians have made themselves household names. They've launched multiple highly successful spin off programs—all similarly structured to the broader *Keeping Up* show—and have introduced countless fashion brands, makeup lines, and perfumes associated with the family name.

But almost all of their business, product and media successes followed their launch onto the celebrity scene.

In 2010, Kim Kardashian earned an estimated yearly income of $7 million. The following year, Kim raked in a reported $18 million profit from her wedding special with basketball player Kris Humphries (that lasted less than a year). And in 2012, Fox News estimated her net worth to be $35 million dollars. [13] Today, *Forbes* estimates that Kim Kardashian is worth $72 Million dollars, earning more than $100 million in the first year of her makeup line, KKW Beauty.[14][15]

And it doesn't stop with Kim. Khloe and Kourtney are both reportedly worth between $35 and $40 million. Kendall Jenner is the highest-paid fashion model in the world and Kylie Jenner, the youngest sister, is widely believed to be the world's youngest billionaire.[16]

But these business careers—for the purposes of this discussion, their talents—followed their rise to public

---

14 Forbes, Kim Kardashian West Profile. July 10, 2020.
15 Schnieder McClain, *Keeping up the Kardashain Brand,"* 10.
16 Friedman and Gonzales, "Kardashian–Jenner Family Worth," April 26, 2020.

renown. They never had to interview for the job. We never assessed their credentials.

As a result, the Kardashians are frequently criticized for lacking talent. In much the same way that they garner attention and build their celebrity, audiences resent the Kardashians for being "famous for being famous." In fact, the debate over whether we should admire or admonish the Kardashian family is one of the more hotly debated subjects in pop culture today.

In a Netflix comedy special, Katherine Ryan asks the crowd to cheer if they like or dislike the Kardashians. The audience roars with hatred for the family and when asked, one woman from the crowd says she doesn't like them because, "They don't do anything."[17]

Don't they? Their entire lives are work.

In Ryan's words, "They do things all the time. You need to follow them on Instagram and you shall see! Kim gets up at 5 a.m., straight in the gym. She eats oatmeal and egg whites. She's, like, basically an athlete. She does that for you."[18]

I, like Katherine Ryan and many other Americans, truly admire the Kardashians. I am not trying to criticize this family's success. I think they saw an opportunity budding and placed a really large bet on what they could make possible with a lot of direct media exposure—and it paid dividends for them.

---

17   Ryan, *Glitter Room*, Netflix, 2019.
18   Ibid.

What concerns me is that we, the fans, are being fed their highly-produced narrative, all while being pressed to overlook the work and production that goes into crafting and maintaining the family's celebrity status.

The Kardashian family represents a first-of-its-kind business model for making money. They piloted the "influencer economy" and, boy, did they succeed. Their enterprise comprises each sister's expertly cultivated social media presence—providing access to the "real" versions of themselves and direct means of interaction with their fans—as well as their incredibly successful commercial product endeavors which span beauty products, fragrances, clothing lines, and lifestyle blogs.

When the end product of this influence is lipstick or shape wear, the societal impact seems relatively harmless.

We are informed consumers purchasing products based on the recommendation of a revered public figure; this is nothing new in the world of advertising. But, to borrow Katherine Ryan's stand up once more: "The Kardashians have Trojan Horsed a lot of important issues into what looks like a vapid reality show. They had an episode on the importance of Planned Parenthood. They had an episode on Gun Control."[19]

So, what should we think of the influencer economy when it moves beyond commercial products and instead becomes an advocacy platform? What should we think when a political point-of-view is being broadcast in a highly-produced,

---

19   Ibid.

well-edited, and often scripted world we are being sold as something raw and real and uncut?

Maintaining influence, is in Kardashian's own words, "a lot of work. . .that might not be so visible to the public eye."[20] If it were more visible, would it change the way we respond to the stories reality stars like the Kardashians are telling?

And, then again, are they really doing anything new? Isn't this how we've interacted with policy makers and business or industry leaders for decades?

THE ART OF APPEALING TO THE MAJORITY

Let's take a quick trip back in time to 2016. The Zika virus has ruined Caribbean tourism. Britain is threatening to leave the European Union. You will never get the sound of Drake singing "I need a one dance" out of your head. My BFF, Jill, has left New York City and moved to the Midwest. Times are tough.

Now, add into the mix that America has just had one of the most divisive election cycles in history, and we are all working through how we should feel when the host of *Celebrity Apprentice* takes over the most powerful office in the country.

Around this time, I took the opportunity to relocate to Singapore for a couple of months to work on a project for one of my clients and, well, it really seemed like a great moment in American culture to move to Asia and be alone for months

---

20   Piazza. *Celebrity, Inc., Pages* 101-103.

on end. I thought that I might be able to escape the weird vibes that characterized every large social event I attended—personal or professional.

I was wrong. In fact, the echo chamber of everything that was happening in the US was even louder when I was abroad, but rather than being surrounded by my peers who were working through the same internal struggle I was, I suddenly became a token American in a foreign country who others could ask the exact question I'd been trying to answer myself, "How did we get here?"

Well, to all the wonderful people I met while in Singapore—I think I'm close to answering your questions. And the inspiration for my answer came from the most unlikely source—Political "Dirty Trickster" Roger Stone.

For anyone who is not familiar with Roger Stone, he is one of the most outlandish political figures of our time. Here's a brief history of his influence on American politics over the past few decades.

Roger Stone is an American political consultant and lobbyist known for his counsel to Republican party candidates. If ever there were to be a cartoon villain for a seedy lobbyist in Washington DC, it would be Roger Stone. The man is perpetually tanned, coiffed, dressed in a three-piece suit, and drinking a martini. And, at any opportunity awarded, he will take off his jacket, vest, and button-down shirt to show off the almost life-size tattoo of Richard Nixon's face located squarely in the center of his shoulder blades.

He is, quite honestly, the perfect subject for a documentary, which is why you will be thrilled to know that there is one about him that you can (and should) watch on Netflix. If not to better understand my own existential turmoil that resulted from watching it, you should at least watch to support my younger sister who is credited as an assistant editor.

It's called *Get Me Roger Stone.*[21]

As stated in the film by political pundit Jeffrey Toobin, Stone is the "Sinister Forrest Gump of American Politics." He pops up at every notable historical moment over the last three decades.[22]

Stone got his start in the industry working on the campaigns for Richard Nixon and Ronald Reagan, then in 1984 formed one of the lead lobbying firms in Washington DC—Black, Manafort, Stone and Kelly. He was involved in a number of political scandals, including the downfall of New York Governor Eliot Spitzer, who Stone implicated in a letter to the FBI detailing the former governor's affairs with prostitutes. He returned to national attention in 2016 when he started serving as an aide on the campaign trail of his longtime friend Donald Trump.

Well, *Get Me Roger Stone*, debuted on Netflix during my time abroad and it incited a frenzy of attention among the Singapore expat community. Most notably when having one of many conversations where I had to awkwardly laugh while

---

21   Bank and DiMauro, *Get Me Roger Stone*, Netflix, 2019.
22   Ibid.

a group of people surrounding me discussed how ridiculous it was that the US elected a reality TV star to the presidency, and one of the friends I had made abroad quoted a Stone soundbite from the film: "Do you think voters, non-sophisticates, make a difference between entertainment and politics? Politics is show business for ugly people."[23]

This quote has really stuck with me since that conversation.

You see, for years I've been a major consumer of pop culture and reality programming. I buy the tabloids at the grocery store checkout line. I sit on the couch most weeknights with my older sister and watch all the Real Housewives fight with each other. But I always separated those experiences from my day-to-day understanding of the world.

I had been operating under the impression that celebrity obsession and reality television were purely extracurricular endeavors. I saw their influence on our economy—it's hard to ignore celebrity endorsements, advertisements, and bespoke products—but I only saw a neutral outcome from that equation. I hadn't considered the possibility that a celebrity could (or would) use their platform and perception to sell us a vision with little to no validation, or potentially manipulate the reality they were living in to make us overlook the staging, framing, and theater that goes into promoting their brands.

But that is exactly what Roger Stone was renowned for being able to do.

---

23   Ibid.

Tucker Carlson, a commentator for Fox News, who was interviewed in the film said it well: "Roger actually gets democracy in a way that most people who cover politics typically don't. Democracy is the process of appealing to the majority."[24]

The 2016 election blew any idealist mentality I once had about the separation of entertainment and policy out of the water, and it really got me thinking. How much of what we read, watch, and hear is curated for us? How much of our news is aggregated to paint a very specific picture of the world we live in and lay the foundation for a future outcome?

Since I began working on this book, I would venture to argue that 100 percent of content with which we interact is designed to communicate a particular point of view. By the very nature of being created by people, it has a subjective perspective. Content always provides a glimpse into the life of the publisher—whether an idyllic image from vacation or a silly picture of friends sharing a night out—it is designed to give consumers a specific impression about the creator.

Celebrities and their publicists have been playing this game for decades; politicians for centuries.

Which led me to question, if something that has always impacted the way society interacts is driving the trends of celebrity and influence we experience today, why does influencer impact suddenly feel so much more acute?

---

24 Ibid.

So, I set out to map the influence economy and its impact on the future of advocacy to determine whether this shift in influence is good, bad, or somewhere in between.

Through this project, I will explore:

What makes a celebrity? Why do some celebrities "make it" while others disappear into obscurity?

What role do celebrities and—by extension—social media influencers play in American culture?

How have changes in the media landscape enabled the rapid rise and expansion of the influence economy?

When nearly everyone has a platform and a microphone, how do we know where to place our trust?

In short, I wrote this book to better understand how those working within the influence economy are leveraging their wide-reaching, captive audiences to sell a point of view—often with a vested interest attached—and make the perspective seem like an obvious choice or part of a worthy trend. I spoke with historians, political theorists, media moguls, and communications professionals who helped me understand where our culture has been and what has changed the way we interact with, not only the media, but also each other.

I started writing this book for anyone who, like me, regularly finds themselves cuddled up on the couch, spending the few, fleeting free moments of our otherwise chaotic days watching celebrities on cable TV enjoy their own leisure time. But, as I researched, I realized that this topic is relevant to anyone who consumes any media. What started as an exploration into reality television has spotlighted for me trends that reach so far beyond reality programming to traditional news broadcasts and beyond, and are—ultimately—woven into to the fabric of American culture and human interaction.

So, if you have ever turned on the news (or *E! News*, again no judgement) and thought to yourself, "How did we get here?" I invite you to explore the cultural foundations for celebrity pop culture and the influence of mass media.

I ask you to bear in mind throughout this book that these opinions are my own, and I hope you will take the time to establish your own perspective on these surreal times.

1

THE RISE OF THE INFLUENCER

———

In June 2019, an Instagram influencer, Marissa Fuchs (now Marissa Grossman) got engaged in an elaborate, live-streamed scavenger hunt engagement that took her from New York to Florida to France. Her engagement in Paris was followed by a wedding ceremony ten minutes later, with 170,000 followers along for the ride.

During the multi-day event, these viewers were glued to their phone screens, anxiously anticipating further details of the fantasy proposal planned by her partner, Gabe Grossman. The hashtag #whereisgabe was trending on multiple social media platforms, as followers questioned where Marissa would go next and whether her future fiancé would actually be waiting for her at the next stop.

But following night two of the Insta-adventure, a presentation deck started circulating the internet, which suggested that Marissa and Gabe had pitched the opportunity to sponsor their engagement and wedding to various brands.

The proposal begins, "This summer, Marissa of @FashionAmbitionist will be pulled into a surprise adventure created by the center of her life, Gabriel. He will remotely ask her to take an unexpected and sentimental journey to him, a journey encompassing [sic] many familiar stops along the way that offer their own unique gifts." It continues, "Throughout this journey, we'll capture heartwarming moments and surprise and delight the soon-to-be bride at every twist, turn and flight! We're pleased to offer your brand the opportunity to align with this momentous occasion and the beautiful cities she will be visiting along the way."[25]

Then it gets tactical: "The FashionAmbitionist team will be releasing long and short form content, as well as Instagram stories and posts detailing each stage of their journey on her channels."[26]

The leak of the pitch deck caused a media frenzy online. Audiences were offended that this emotional roller coaster they had been riding on Instagram might be staged.

In an interview between Kelsey Hodgkin of advertising agency Deutsch Los Angeles and reporter Taylor Lorenz, the emerging authority on all things social media and the internet, Hodgkin said she was "unsurprised that the couple would try to make money off such a momentous life event.

---

25   Lorenz, "Welcome to the Era of Branded Engagements," June 20, 2019.
26   Ibid.

Celebrities, reality stars, and other influencers already monetize their weddings, their pregnancies, and their breakups; an engagement is par for the course."[27]

"I think it's completely insane, but very of the moment we're living in now," Hodgkin told Lorenz of Fuchs's proposal. "Influencer marketing is a free-for-all at the moment. Everyone is like, 'How far can I push it?' ... This current state is unsustainable. The more influencers are fabricating scenarios for brands to be part of, the less influential they become."[28]

But, on the other side of the coin, Lorenz argues that even if Fuchs had a hand in planning her engagement and wedding adventure, her fans likely wouldn't back away from her channels because, "Influencers have a unique bond with their audiences, who have proved to be extremely loyal."[29]

Advertising executive Bryan Pedersen, who additionally spoke with Lorenz in her development of this article, stated, "The audience doesn't just see an influencer as an [entertainment] channel or celebrity; they see them as a friend. And if it's a friend, you're going to forgive anything."[30]

It is exactly this sentiment that raises red warning flags around the influencer economy for many, myself included.

---

27 Ibid.
28 Ibid.
29 Ibid.
30 Ibid.

KEEPING UP AND GETTING REAL

I've admitted it before, and I'll admit it again: I am a habitual consumer of reality television. I often cannot wait to get home to turn on Bravo and catch up with my "friends" on the *Real Housewives of* multiple cities and you can best believe I am *Keeping Up With the Kardashians*. And I believe this is exactly what the producers creating this content want us to feel for the characters they promote. There is something in the pseudo-realism of reality television and Instagram content that encourages this personal attachment and trust.

When discussing his own experience consuming paid influencer content, Sam Sanders from NPR noted that the imagery often "blurs the line between real and fake...I'll be scrolling Instagram, and I'm seeing posts from my friends, you know, at the park, with their babies and their dogs. And then I see another post from an influencer that kind of looks the same way, but they're pushing me a product. And I don't know. As just, like, a layperson, as a consumer, sometimes I worry about the very premise."[31]

We've created a unique application of capitalism through which we can easily and legally monetize ourselves. Instagram influencers are selling a performance, a perception, and a lifestyle. They curate their daily lives for the entertainment of others—in many ways taking on both the role of subject and producer of reality television—to expand their reach and cultivate trust with their followers. And, through it all, package up their lives in such a way that, as Sanders mentions, "every moment of [their] waking day[s], can be an advertising message."[32]

---

31 Sanders, "The New Celebrity," September 10, 2019.
32 Ibid.

That voyeuristic view, however, is exactly the value that reality programming offers.

Throughout most of the program, we're invited into the private lives of the rich, powerful, beautiful, and interesting. We see their celebrations, their fights, and share in their heartbreaks. We've been present for proposals and divorce proceedings, and we've welcomed their children into the world and watched them send them off to college. But, throughout these private moments, we're reminded that we're watching something captured for our entertainment.

"Confessional" style interviews between characters and producers call our attention to those off-camera influencers that have been present for all we've just seen, but social media doesn't allow for that same peek behind the curtain.

Platforms like Facebook and Instagram feed into our inherently human inclination toward nosiness and gossip. The reality of it is nothing new—we have always been a community-oriented species and nothing unites us more than the ability to talk about someone else.

In many ways, social media storytelling serves a similar function to theater and performance.

For centuries, we have viewed theater as a reflective art form. Ancient Greek philosopher Aristotle wrote in his *Poetics* that theater could deliver purification and healing qualities— catharsis—to the spectators, who are in turn meant to assess performance themes for direction and reflection on society.

We look to influencers and celebrities for that same purpose. We want to see ourselves in them, and as such we provide more slack that we might traditionally give someone that has broken society's faith. Their admissions of their own failings are seen as virtues—real, raw, unfiltered, relatable.

It is precisely their relatability that makes influencers so successful. They are different from our traditional celebrities in that they do not outwardly present some unique gift or talent (that might make it challenging for the public to see a reflection of itself in their actions). In many ways, we respect them specifically *for* their lack of talent.

On the other side of the coin, we often see these influencers as somewhat disposable assets. We regularly use them as scapegoats, challenging cultural insensitivity they reflect when it doesn't match our own idealism; or worse, when it highlights something in our culture we're embarrassed to say we've done ourselves, but more on that later.

Influencers or—as USC professor of sociology Elizabeth Currid-Halkett refers to them—"talentless celebrities" aim to achieve fame first, and then put it to work for their brands.[33]

I think we need to define a couple of terms to prevent myself from categorically offending an entire class of celebrities I follow. For ease, I will borrow a handful of definitions from Currid-Halkett's work.

---

33   Currid-Halkett, "Starstruck," Kindle Location 431.

- **Talent**: Talent describes a person's inherent abilities, whether that is running at faster speeds, acting more convincingly, writing lyrics that resonate, or orating with conviction.
- **Fame**: Fame refers purely to renown. It is a measure of the sum of people who have heard a particular person's name and can connect it meaningfully with something else—their face, brand, voice, ideas, talents.
- **Celebrity**: The phenomenon that society collectively cares about a particular person for reasons that outweigh (or have nothing to do with) their talent or deserved fame.

We can also assess the extent of an individual's celebrity by looking at the "celebrity-residual."[34] **Celebrity residual** considers the difference between how much we as a populace *should* care about a person (as determined by their measurable talent) and the amount that we *actually* do (as determined by their fame—photographs, news stories, mind share). [35]

Stick with me. I'll give you an example.

Michael Jordan is certainly famous. His basketball career is renowned worldwide, if not only for his abilities but also for the fact that he lends his name to a leading line of sneakers designed to play his sport. But what does the common consumer know of Jordan beyond the court? He has almost non-existent celebrity residual.

---

34 Ibid.
35 Ibid.

Now consider the fame of Tristan Thompson. He acquired renown playing basketball for the Cleveland Cavaliers, but truly stepped into the limelight when he left his girlfriend (who was in her third trimester carrying their child) to date reality star Khloe Kardashian.

Tristan became a true celebrity when he and Khloe, who had only been together for a brief period of time, announced that they were expecting a baby. But what *really* expanded his celebrity came next. Because, guess what? Tristan cheated on Khloe during her third-trimester, and Kardashian fans around the country came for Thompson with torches and pitchforks.

Social media exploded with memes portraying Thompson as the most-hated person in the entire world. A message wishing "good night to everyone on the planet, except Tristan Thompson," went viral.[36]

Jokes emerged that Thompson never runs faster than when his girlfriend hits her third trimester. And you can bet that today, people know Tristan for his associations with the Kardashian family more so than his position on the Cleveland Cavaliers.

Therefore, Tristan "Third-Trimester" Thompson is a celebrity. He is talented, for sure. But his renown extends beyond his basketball career, with Kardashian fans tracking the details of his romantic relationships and sparking high volumes of

---

36 Lawrence, "Support to Khloe Kardashian amid cheating scandal," April 12, 2018.

social chatter whenever he steps out of line. He, thus, has considerably high celebrity residual.

So how would one turn their celebrity residual into influential power? To understand how, there's only one family you need to study: the Kardashians.

MANUFACTURING CELEBRITY

Kim Kardashian, her siblings, and her momager, Kris, have been making headlines for years. But considering that she's not an actress, a singer, or a socialite, then what exactly was it that made Kim Kardashian famous in the first place?

Simple: she wanted to become a celebrity, so she made it happen.

In an article exploring the exact question of why Kim Kardashian is famous, Showbiz Cheat Sheet reporter Amanda Harding wrote, "Kim Kardashian represents a brand of celebrities whose fame just breeds more fame, often for no particular reason or because of any discernible talent."[37] It's a genuinely interesting phenomenon.

Kim Kardashian, and other "famous for being famous" stars have built celebrity comprised almost entirely of "celebrity residual."

The Kardashian name first came into the public realm when Robert Kardashian served as a member of accused murderer

---

37   Harding, "Why Is Kim Kardashian West Famous?." March 5, 2019.

O.J. Simpson's legal defense team in 1994. At the time, the Kardashian children—Kim, Kourtney, Khloe, and Rob—were still very young. After the case the family would fall back out of public consciousness for another decade, while the kids grew older.

From 2004–2006, Kim Kardashian entered the Hollywood social scene. As a stylist for Brandy and close friend of Paris Hilton who occasionally appeared on Hilton's reality TV show, *The Simple Life*, Kim started to build her image as a member of the Hollywood elite.

In July 2006, Kim and her sisters open their first store, DASH, in their hometown of Calabasas, California. Kim was the primary face for the brand, leaning into her expertise as Brandy's stylist to build the popularity of the store.

But 2007 is when things really got interesting.

In February 2007, a home sex tape that Kim filmed with then boyfriend, Ray J, leaked on TMZ online. A porn company called Vivid Entertainment bought the rights to the video and released the film as a 41-minute home movie, called *Kim Kardashian, Superstar.*

And so, she was.

In October 2007, the first episode of *Keeping Up With the Kardashians* aired on E!. The episode showed the modern family celebrating the anniversary of the Kardashian's mother, Kris, and step-father, Bruce Jenner. Kim leans into her sexy image and gifts her mother and Bruce a stripper pole, which she has installed in Kris' excessively large walk-in closet.

There is, however, only so far a sex symbol can reach when it comes to influence. Kim wanted to move beyond the covers of *Cosmopolitan*, so she needed to pivot her image.

She did exactly that in December 2007, surprisingly by posing nude for Playboy. In her Playboy interview, Kim begins to establish herself as Hollywood's voice of body positivity. She shared with the Playboy team that she was nervous about the shoot, because, "You always see the typical skinny models and I'm not that and I'm proud not to be that."[38] She paired her curves and a highly confident nude photo with a vulnerable admission that she—too—sometimes feels insecure, and in a single interview flipped the narrative that Hollywood was creating for her.

Due in large part to Kim's rising celebrity, the first season of *Keeping Up With the Kardashians* was a resounding success. E! launched the second season only six months after the first, in addition to many, many spin offs (including 2009's *Kourtney and Khloe Take Miami*, to celebrate the launch of the sister's second DASH store opening in the city, and followed by *Kourtney and Kim Take New York* to chronicle the opening of DASH NYC in 2011).

The Kardashian reality TV empire reigns to this day.

---

38 Baxter-Wright, "How did Kim Kardashian Actually Get Famous?" September 27, 2017

The incredible continued success of the Kardashian family has given way to an entire "cultural phenomenon which is like a tidal wave taking over the world," Viral Nation co-founder, Joe Gagliese notes in an interview with NPR. "And this isn't just here. I think it's the lightest in the U.S. and Canada... Like, you should see it in China. You should see it in places like Italy and the U.K. and Latin America, Brazil. We've created the new celebrity."[39]

And it is this pervasive cultural shift that has Gagliese convinced that the explosion of the influencer economy does not indicate a bubble that will soon burst, but rather a shift in the way people interact. He notes, "I find it very hard to believe, with that undertone, that influencers would go away. Now, can marketing with influencers be affected? One hundred percent. Could there be new social channels, and Instagram goes down one day? One hundred percent. Like, I think there's going to be huge disruption in the space from a marketing perspective, from a use perspective, from a platform perspective—all that stuff. But I think influencer is the new status symbol of humanity."[40]

Well, Joe, you're not wrong, but it's nothing new. Influencer has always been the status symbol of humanity—we're simply experiencing a different wave of influencer renown than previously known.

---

39 Sanders, "The New Celebrity," September 10, 2019.
40 Ibid.

2

CELEBRITY IS A
SOCIAL CONSTRUCT

———

I know I said I'd look back into the annals of history, but that can be a little boring. So, first, let's take a look at the original "celebutante"—Paris Hilton.

It's the beginning of a new millennium. Paris Hilton sprung onto the scene during a cultural moment that celebrated excess, and she was a perfect idol for cultural obsession. The product of one of the richest families in America with bleach blonde hair, long legs, a willingness to show a lot of skin, and, finally, a ditzy persona she was willing to cash in on, Paris quickly climbed the ranks of celebrity.

She was a well-known party girl—frequently photographed drinking in trendy clubs, dancing on tables, and fighting with other socialites. She met her foil in Tara Reid, a young, blonde, blue eyed, incredibly thin actress, who similarly loved to party (and in fact had made a career out of it). They were a natural pair. Reid and Hilton were regularly photographed together at nightclubs and perpetuated an image of a wild scene only accessible to the young, rich, and famous.

Both were plagued by very public stumbles in the media. Both "accessorize[d] with indecent exposure. (Paris was caught on camera without underwear and Tara's dress fell off, exposing a breast). Both are seen about town...drunk, dancing on tabletops, getting in fights, falling into limousines."[41]

But one fateful night in 2006, the tides shifted and Reid fell out of favor.

See, following the conclusion of her reality show, *The Simple Life*, and a major falling out with her best friend Nicole Richie, Paris Hilton was in need of a sidekick and decided to host auditions. At the time, Reid appeared to be a natural fit for the role. But negative media attention has a way of spoiling plans for aspiring celebrities and, unfortunately, Reid was drawing the wrong kind of attention. At the same time, a new friendship was budding between Hilton and another born-into-wealth socialite, closet organizer and stylist Kim Kardashian.

Kim Kardashian had been friends with Hilton since they were "young girls," but was otherwise relatively unknown in Hollywood, which makes her rise to fame even more impressive.

And what's more? The moment that Kardashian stole Reid's piece of the socialite pie is caught on camera and played relentlessly on TMZ.

---

41   Currid-Halkett, "Starstruck," Kindle Location 336.

In the video, Reid is in line for the Hyde Lounge nightclub when a bouncer, with whom it appears Reid is very familiar—in fact, friendly—informs her that he cannot let her into the club. Then, from the other direction, Hilton struts up to the velvet rope arm-in-arm with Kim Kardashian. The two walk directly in front of Reid, Hilton looks Reid in the eye and snubs her as the pair of newly-minted best friends enter the club Reid has been barred from.

And so it goes. Hilton and Kardashian go on to become cultural icons and build formidable commercial empires: The Paris brand (separate from the Hilton Hotel fortune) is worth millions, following the success of Hilton's perfume, clothing, and jewelry lines. Kardashian, too, has launched fashion lines, makeup lines, perfumes, television series, and more.

Conversely, Reid is relegated to the Hollywood D-List and regularly mocked, if she is thought of at all, occasionally making headlines for poor plastic surgery, indecent exposure, and alcohol abuse.

All this because mind share is a zero sum game. If someone is gaining popularity, that means someone else is losing it.

IT'S ALL ABOUT NETWORKING

The Kim Kardashian / Tara Reid winner-take-all story has played out many times among the Hollywood elite.

To understand how to build and maintain fame, you must first recognize that in popular culture, celebrities do not become celebrities because *we* want them to be famous. *They* need to make a conscious decision to build and reinforce their own brands, and then they need to work constantly to maintain and expand their renown.

"A fundamental quality of celebrity is that celebrities are celebrities because they spend time with other celebrities, reinforcing the belief that they truly are different from you and me," Elizabeth Currid-Halkett mentions in her research into the social networks of celebrities.[42] "It's not that we anoint people...they decide that they want to be stars too. They buy a ticket to the lottery," she explains.[43]

It's worth noting, however, that the lottery they enter isn't a game of chance. They can tip the scale in their own favor.

If nothing else, celebrity is a product of our cultural industries—including the arts, publishing, and media. Examining how one might establish and build celebrity therefore requires a look at how one breaks into these taste-driven cultural industries at large.

In her earlier research, Currid-Halkett analyzed the art industry and why so many starving artists moved to New York— where the price of a tiny studio apartment would require the artist to work multiple jobs and afford no time or space to complete their work, and what she notes many explained to her is that a huge part of work in cultural industries requires "interacting with the people who legitimize work."[44]

42 Currid-Halkett, "Starstruck," Kidle Location 1387.
43 USC Price, "Starstruck Literary Luncheon," May 12, 2011.
44 Ibid.

A similar interaction is required in establishing celebrity and renown in Hollywood; we see this play out in interactions between celebrities themselves.

Now, Currid-Halkett was researching celebrity in 2011, which is basically ancient history in popular culture, but one thing that this time in history enabled her to research (which I'm not sure would be possible today) was that social media was just beginning to catch on as a celebrity communications platform. That meant that Currid-Halkett didn't need to analyze self-published images from celebrities in her research. Instead, she was able to leverage the Getty Images library of celebrity photos as a data set that helped her tag the locations and events at which celebrities interacted. She mapped these interactions and plotted celebrity networks. Through this work, she was able to identify that while we—the rest of the world—are connected to each other by about 6 degrees of separation on average, celebrities are connected to each other by 3.26 degrees of separation, based solely on their appearances at industry events and mixers.[45]

Based on her observations, celebrity begets celebrity.

So, with this in mind, Kim Kardashian attaching her platform to Paris Hilton's during a moment when Paris was at the top of the socialite network and raking in money from brand partnerships, media collaborations, and her own products was a brilliant networking decision.

The mastermind behind it all was Kris Jenner.

---

45   Ibid.

While *The Simple Life* was airing, Hilton's manager at the time, Jason Moore, had developed a marketing plan for Hilton that would turn her from socialite to business mogul. Reporter Sarah Frier details the Kardashian-Jenner-Hilton plot in her book, *No Filter.* "Moore tried to turn everything Hilton did into a moneymaking venture...In a society without social media or the iPhone to show fans' enthusiasm, Moore would bring his own camcorder around the world to create video reels of Hilton arriving in new cities and launching products, so they could edit and present the footage to potential business partners. By seeing Hilton around her enthusiastic fans, brands understood the value of attaching her name to their projects."[46]

Knowing that they had a show in the works and a clothing brand to expand, Jenner sought to build the visibility of her family—beginning with Kim.

"Jenner realized that the fastest way to achieve fame was by being associated with more famous people...So in 2006, before *Keeping Up With the Kardashians* began airing, she called Moore to ask if Hilton and Kardashian could appear together more often, as her daughter was looking to build a clothing business called DASH. Kardashian was a much curvier brunette, who would appeal to a different kind of consumer entirely, Moore thought. He told Jenner it would not be a problem."[47]

So really, Tara Reid can blame Kris Jenner for her very public demotion to the D-list. As many on social media have said: the Devil works hard but Kris Jenner works harder.

---

46   Frier, "No Filter," Pages 136-137.

47   Ibid.

Having much stronger credibility in social science and statistics than I do, Currid-Halkett's explanation of the reinforcing ecosystem of celebrity networks may be more persuasive than my singular example from the brilliant marketing mind of Kris Jenner.

Currid-Halkett also finds that the close connections within celebrity are mirrored in other tightly knit industries, like finance and publishing, and often result in interactions that can lead to career promotions and connections to more important people within these industries. But there are more niches in networking to advance a career in an industry like finance or publishing. A single relationship can be nurtured over time to open new opportunities down the line.

It doesn't work quite the same way in celebrity industries.

I mentioned that Currid-Halkett found in her research that the broader class of celebrities is connected by 3.26 degrees of separation, and the connections get tighter as you move up through the celebrity ranks. Celebrity C- and B-listers are connected by 2.5 and 2.22 degrees respectively.[48] The A-list is connected by 1.6 degrees of separation, but making your way into the A-list isn't a natural trajectory; it doesn't happen by nurturing one strategic relationship in hopes of being invited to the party. It has traditionally required "a quantum leap into the A-list, such as winning an Oscar or marrying an A-lister."[49]

---

48   Currid-Halkett, "Starstruck," Kindle Location 1567.
49   Ibid,

So, to those unlikely to win an Oscar in the near future, establishing and building celebrity requires a different motivation in networking: being seen by others. So, for someone who wants "to become a celebrity...there is no better network than befriending people who are constantly photographed by the media."[50] You might not make your way into the official A-list, but it will seem externally to others that you have. And, at the end of the day, isn't that all that really matters?

Using Google News hits as a data set to assess the most discussed celebrities, Currid-Halkett also found that the most-talked about celebrities—those with high celebrity residual—had social networks similar to Hollywood's A-list actors. She described her findings stating, "these most talked about celebrities tend to be connected to lots of people, attend lots of events and have just as close connections among their friends as A-list Hollywood actors do among themselves."[51]

But this doesn't happen without work.

These fully residual stars attend almost 80 percent more events than the Hollywood A-listers do. They can never take the night off without risking the loss of mind share or, even worse, looking like they weren't invited.[52]

In this regard, you can compare them to the starving artists attending gallery openings in New York City, hoping to catch their big break. By being visible at these events, aspiring stars

---

50 USC Price, "Starstruck Literary Luncheon," May 12, 2011.
51 Currid-Halkett, "Starstruck," Location 1590.
52 Ibid.

have the opportunity to meet more celebrities who can help grow their careers, mingle with brand marketing leads who can help secure sponsor gigs and endorsement deals, and bond with lead designers at major labels to get a foot in the door toward becoming the face for a leading house of fashion.

The more these residual stars are seen among tastemakers—designers, producers, and other such Hollywood gatekeepers—the more their credibility as a true star grows. Work at this long enough, and they might just be able to make that quantum leap into the A-list.

When you think about these celebrity social butterflies, eagerly attending industry events to have their photo taken and splashed across tabloid pages, it all feels eerily familiar, doesn't it?

I've never had the opportunity to walk a red carpet, so I have no like-for-like experience with such industry events. But yet, I know the residual celebrity personally. You do too.

This person knows everyone in town and is somehow involved in every committee. They show up at every party, but no one is totally clear who invited them. They aren't a disruptive presence. No one groans when they walk in, but even the host is questioning whether or not they'd actually been sent an invitation.

In a time of Instagram, this person is even more visible and confusing. They hop into your group photo before you even know they're there, and it would be far too rude to ask them to step out. So instead, they will be cemented into social media record as you upload the post, finesse the caption, and tag them.

Their loosely connected networks see them popping up at all of these various events and are surprised by the diverse mix of cliques into which they have been inducted. Wait, they know my friend's friend from high school? Is that them at my ex-boyfriend's birthday party? They're on vacation *again*? With *who*?

Yeah. You know this person. And now you know what they're up to. If they stop showing up at all of these events and mingling with all of these cliques they sacrifice associations, and without their visible network, what would be left?

3

ACHIEVING INFLUENCE

———

Have you ever been asked to read *Beowulf*? (No one has ever read it by choice.) I ask because Beowulf himself was an aspiring influencer, leveraging his celebrity residual to make his mark on the world.

The Old English epic focuses on a war hero, Beowulf, known for being: *"The man most gracious and fair-minded / Kindest to his people and **keenest to win fame**."*[53]

In an op-ed published in *WIRED*, Virginia Heffernan observed that *"Beowulf*, was, if not 'famous for being famous' (in the 1960s phrase), something weirder still: famous for wanting to be famous. Beowulf's strengths are not chiefly bravery or even victories in battle; he is renowned precisely for his thirst for fame."[54]

And can you blame him? That desire for recognition shouldn't feel foreign to most modern Americans.

———

53 Heffernan, "Fame on the Internet," August 20, 2019.
54 Ibid.

He was being sent into battle and undertaking tasks of actual epic proportion, and just wanted some attention and praise for his epic feats. I have to assume that many of our real-life war heroes, leaders, politicians, and, yes, celebrities of the past have been driven by similar motivations.

They want to establish themselves among the peer set they most admire.

I spent a lot of time in college reading about the social, political, and economic foundations of America, and I keep coming back to this idea that at its founding, America was a nation inspired by the idea that an individual could be whomever he wanted (whomever she and they wanted followed later). I believe it's that right to freedom and individual pursuit of happiness, rooted in a rejection of aristocratic class, that makes our desire for praise and recognition so strong. It's been ingrained within our spirit over generations of being told that, as Americans, we don't need to play the hand we were dealt. We can control our own destiny. Our hard work will be rewarded.

It is in this tradition of social mobility in which social hierarchies thrive. Our economy is underpinned by a deeply-rooted meritocracy, and that meritocracy created for us the exact hierarchy in social status we once rebelled against. The roots of fame are particularly important because understanding celebrity culture first requires an assessment of society and communal structures. Because, at its core, celebrity is an organizing principle.

In his book, *The Frenzy of Renown*, Leo Braudy examined the role of celebrity throughout history. Braudy claims that every era has its own famous celebrities, and in most cases, the celebrities' paths to fame mirror those of eras past.

We have seen fame manifest as "individuals have sought to bring themselves to the attention of others and, not incidentally, have thereby gained power over them. But few self-assertions, especially those staged in public, are ever wholly original."[55]

In a time of limited media, individuals needed to perform some kind of noteworthy task or demonstrate some universal value to society in order to build renown, spread largely by word of mouth. So, frequently, aspiring leaders would mirror the acts of legends that captured society's imagination. In his assessment of fame over the history of Western civilization, Braudy notes that Alexander the Great imitated the legends of the Gods and War Heroes, like Achilles, in his campaign for renown. Julius Caesar mirrored Alexander. Their rise to renown and to rule was rooted in perceived civic virtue; this in turn allowed them to take positions leading society and building throngs of followers.

Some of the most famous individuals to date—those whose portraits grace the pages of our history books—rose to renown through actions attributed to their civic virtues: their contributions to society, whether in the form of scholarship and government (as with Socrates) or in battle (as with Caesar) were seen as actions taken to support the community. And publicity around the individual was rooted in celebration of the contribution to the community. These

---

55   Braudy, "Frenzy of Renown," Page 3.

heroic acts or contributions garnered not only praise and admiration, but frequently were met with leadership roles and rights within the community. Their fame paved the path to their power and vice versa, in a self-perpetuating and self-perpetuated cycle.

It's within this context that I best understand the phenomenon of the relative celebrity (another term defined by USC professor Elizabeth Currid-Halkett).[56] What is popularity if not small-scale celebrity? The most popular in our hometowns are celebrities relative to the rest of us.

I bet you're already thinking of that person from your past who could seemingly do no wrong and were constantly lauded for everything they did.

The older sibling who was head cheerleader, valedictorian, class president, adored by parents, teachers, and peers alike.

And, on the other side of the coin, you recognize that person's younger sibling who can seemingly do no right. The stereotypical loser—head of the AV club, small social circle, badly dressed, and frequently mocked. One cannot exist without the other.

The relative celebrities in a high school setting are "The Plastics."

For my peers, *Mean Girls* was the comedy of a generation. If you are one of the few who has not seen *Mean Girls*—stop reading now. Go watch *Mean Girls*. This can wait.

---

56   USC Price, "Starstruck Literary Luncheon," May 12, 2011.

But, if you don't have time to watch, here is a quick overview. Cady Heron (Lindsey Lohan) moves back to the United States with her parents following a childhood living in Africa, where her parents worked as research zoologists. She is plopped into an average American high school with absolutely no social or cultural context, and her observations about the way teenagers operate consistently relate to the way wild animals behave on the African plains.

Much of the story revolves around a popular clique, called "The Plastics," who—enabled by wealth, beauty, and exclusivity—are the social directors of the entire high school (teachers and administrators included). They sit above their peers because they run in circles that only really include themselves.

And, as was stated in the film, being part of the Plastics "was like being famous. People looked at you all the time, and everybody just knew stuff about you."[57] And, beyond the buzz that surrounds them, they influence the trends of the entire school.

To try and embarrass the queen bee, Regina George, Cady and her friends cut holes in the chest of her tank top. Regina wears it out of the locker room with confidence and in the next scene you see every female student and teacher walking through the hallway with holes cut out of their tops.

Once Cady becomes a member of the Plastics, she too is a trendsetter.

---

57 Waters dir., *Mean Girls*, 2004.

"I saw Cady Heron wearing army pants and flip flops, so I bought army pants and flip flops," one schoolmate confesses to the camera.[58]

Any girl who was still in high school during the height of the *Mean Girls* phenomenon will be able to relate to this conversation:

"*Mean Girls* was based on my school."

"Everyone says that."

"But seriously, we had something exactly like this happen a few years back when...," and so on.

This relevance and resonance can be attributed to two things:

1. Tina Fey's genius.
2. The ubiquity of the "relative celebrity."

The relative celebrity makes its way into nearly every sitcom, network drama, romantic comedy, or teen-movie.

It's Tim Riggins from *Friday Night Lights*: the captain of the high school football team and lovable screw-up you just can't help but root for. Or Caroline from *Sixteen Candles*: the beautiful prom queen who throws crazy parties and dates Jake Ryan, the most handsome boy in school. Or even Uncle Jesse from *Full House*: the super-cool, guitar playing,

---

58   Ibid.

bachelor (turned family man) with amazing hair and his own catchphrase.

These small-scale, everyday celebrities consume conversations and have us—their extended audiences—ready to say "have mercy" every time they give us something new and scandalous to talk about.

Today, our relative celebrities are not limited to the small-town spheres of influence they once ruled. The characters from *Friday Night Lights*, *Sixteen Candles*, and *Full House* are easy-to-unpack examples of relative celebrities because they only existed within the boundaries of their own manufactured communities.

But with the rise of social media and the internet, our relative celebrities have a much wider audience, giving everyone, everywhere new windows into the lives of the home-town famous.

Now, I am not suggesting that your hometown Cady Heron will make her way into our history books, or even onto the Instagram Discover page—but I know that some are trying.

Today, we all carry fully-fledged mass media ecosystems around in our pockets. So, in lieu of celebrity earned by legendary feats, we can create renown on our own, building influential, curated personas supported by well-selected photo filters. We can promote our networks with visuals of the events we've been invited to, tag the people we want to be associated with, and through comments on Facebook walls and Instagram posts.

Relative celebrity is taking root in our own private lives. So, while it may seem frivolous to throw attention toward the *Real Housewives of Orange County* and support an enterprise of shameless self-promotion on television, should we be asking the same questions of whether we should "like" daily posts on Instagram that essentially accomplish the same end? To an extent, it's too late to ask the question. We've already accepted that practice as common place.

So, before you ridicule those of us watching reality TV, consider that Braudy—in his assessment of the history of fame—wrote that to dismiss the societal impact of celebrity culture would be an oversight and to suggest that any such celebrity is simply popular for surface level reasons and to cast them off as simply 'famous for being famous' would be to "ignore the importance of celebrity in shaping the values of our society."[59]

TAKING CONTROL OF YOUR OWN NARRATIVE

"We live in a society bound together by the talk of fame," Braudy writes.[60] Or, said differently, celebrities—and relative celebrities—provide we mere average folk with a unifying conversational device. Celebrities support water cooler chit-chat in the office and provide safe conversation-drivers at family dinner parties.

Instead of feigning interest in local humidity levels over the past week, we can shift to talking points provided by our

---

59 Braudy, "Frenzy of Renown," Page 9.
60 Braudy, "Frenzy of Renown," Preface vii

favorite tabloids—a royal wedding, a pregnancy scandal, a devastating breakup, or an entertaining anecdote shared in an interview. The most intimate details of celebrities' lives save us from having to talk about our own.

As a society, we are drawn to collective experiences, whether that is going to see a production together or gathering over brunch to chat about last night's spectacle. Economists call these relationships "network externalities," or the effects a product or service has on a user while others are using the same or compatible products or services. Positive network externalities exist if the benefit of consuming something increases with each additional person who also participates.[61]

In casual terms—if you watched *Schitt's Creek* before it went viral, it doesn't matter. But if you haven't watched *Schitt's Creek* after it went viral, everyone will know and probably judge you.

Modern celebrities have tuned in to this cultural phenomenon. They have analyzed the platforms fueling conversation, have developed strategies to take control of their own public personas, and are cashing in.

Unfortunately for Paris Hilton, the height of her fame and influence came right as the social media landscape as we know it was budding. During that moment, "Hilton's carefully controlled images and videos fueled her business. So, when digital platforms like YouTube and iTunes eventually

---

61   Currid-Halkett, "Starstruck," Kindle Location 2273.

reached out for the opportunity to feature Hilton's videos or music for nothing in return, [her publicist, Jason] Moore dismissed them."[62]

But Kim Kardashian was still building her fame when Twitter launched and realized that she had an opportunity to build her image using social media as a direct line of communication to fans. Her extended family then realized that they had an opportunity with social media to take control of their own external narratives. [63]

Through direct interactions with her followers, Kim Kardashian is able to refine and nurture her public persona. Her willingness to let followers behind-the-scenes of her life has helped her build a following that today numbers more than 65.5 million users.

Kardashian's activity on Twitter—and later on Instagram—is a unique blend of personal tidbits, lifestyle updates, direct interaction with fans, interactions with other celebrities (frequently her own sisters), messages directing traffic to her other online platforms (in the early years, her blog, now to her web page KKW.com, where you can purchase her many product lines), and finally overtly promotional tweets.[64]

According to Amanda Schnieder McClain, who studied a full year of Kim Kardashian's Twitter activity to identify patterns in her posts wrote, "She broadcasts where she is and what

62   Frier, "No Filter," Pages 137-138.
63   Ibid.
64   McClain, "Keeping UP the Kardashian Brand," Pages 78-84.

she's doing, posts self-taken photos of herself and her friends, interacts with fans and is seemingly candid about inconsequential aspects of her life...Kim's use of Twitter positions her as equal to everyone else able to utilize the service, modifying her celebrity status. Concurrently, some of the content of her tweets validates her celebrity status."[65]

Kim Kardashian was, in many ways, the first of an era of Democratic Celebrities.

ALL THE WORLD'S A STAGE

New media, technologies, social platforms, and reality television programming have perpetuated all forms of celebrity, and—in turn—have reduced barriers to entry unlike any other point in history. Our reality stars and influencers have formed a new class: democratic celebrities. They have circumvented the normal vetting process that typically keeps us out of Hollywood, and that is part of their appeal.

As Currid-Halkett observed in her book on fame and celebrity, "the democracy of dream-achievement provoked the leitmotif of the decade: the culture and triumph of amateurism. The feeling that people without experience, expert knowledge, skill, learning or aptitude had something extra, something special to offer."[66] Our desire to believe that we, too, could achieve some level of super-stardom has made these democratic celebrities just as legitimate as their talented peers.

---

65 Ibid.
66 Currid-Halkett, "Starstruck," Kindle Location 2816.

In exchange for our support, the democratic celebrities (and aspiring celebrities) are willing to "trade their intimate moments—some seemingly mortifying and embarrassing—for the chance that the world might take notice of them... The banal details of one's personal life are the currency of contemporary celebrity."[67]

They use their platforms to make fans identify with them, rather than simply adore them from afar. And, in fact, their success depends upon fans and followers identifying with them. And we do. We really do.

I don't know about you, but for me the most quintessential phrase of the 2000's has to be, "We should have a TV show." I can remember saying this phrase at nearly every stage of my life so far.

When I was younger, I was so jealous of Allison Stoner on Disney 411. Just like Allison, I watched all of the Disney programming. But, while I sat in my living room in Ho-Ho-Kus, New Jersey, Allison got to broadcast into the homes of kids like me around the country, while she talked with the Disney stars about their experiences making Disney Channel Original Movies.

Why not me? My cousins and I would broadcast our own talk shows from our play theater sets in the basement, and we were pretty entertaining to our ten-year-old selves. At the time I thought that others would have enjoyed the content. But, if child-generated content on YouTube and TikTok are at

---

67   USC Price, "Starstruck Literary Luncheon," May 12, 2011.

all indicative of the types of content my cousins and I would have captured a decade ago, I honestly thank the good Lord that we did not have a TV show.

Later in life, as I was at college in Washington DC, living with five of my closest friends, going to class during the day, and drinking $13 vodka more frequently than anyone really should have, I was having the time of my life, and as a result was again convinced that we could have a TV show.

But, now a connoisseur of reality programming I can say—without a doubt—that we could not have had a TV show. I love my friends and I cherish my years in college, but that would have been the most boring program in reality TV history.

Seriously. It would have been worse that *What Would Ryan Lochte Do?* on E!, where the producers often had to animate drawings of the weird things he said during confessional style interviews to try and force a bit of excitement into his life of swimming and drinking at clubs.

Trust me, guys, we were hilarious, but we did not have the kind of entertaining lifestyles (nor did we have the budget to support said lifestyles) that would have kept audiences engaged for more than about fifteen minutes of content. Very few would have appreciated watching us eat hummus at 2 a.m., talk about our fun night at the same bar we went to the night before, and then crawl into bed to prepare to do the same thing the next day.

What I find interesting about all of this, though, is that this is not a unique sentiment. To this day, when I am out to dinner in New York I can hear groups having the same conversation I once had. "Oh my God, you're so right. We *should* have a TV show."

I truly believe this idea is perpetuated by the influencers who have broken through themselves. As they spotlight the ways they circumvented traditional vetting processes, our democratic celebrities make it seem like we all could do the same, that makes us *want* to do the same.

Their status and successes seem attainable and therefore, it inoculates them against the common attack toward American socialites that they are "entitled" and therefore undeserving of our attentions.

These democratic stars share a view into the traditions of celebrity and fame—the architecture that first made us revere celebrities and keep them in a class of their own—and make it seem to the rest of us that these desirable perks are not entirely out of our reach. This causes them to appear at once, and paradoxically, both accessible and exclusive. And it is their engagement with that paradox that makes us support them so strongly. We believe that we have played a role in establishing their celebrity, and we happily accept the responsibility of furthering their fame, but we'll just as quickly take support away from a star if we believe that they have stepped out of line.

4

YOU'RE CANCELLED.

———

Emily Dickinson said it best in the 1700s: "Fame is a fickle food."[68]

Its fickle nature, however, expands rather dramatically when the fame in question is entirely defined by celebrity residual fueled by democratic appeal. Because just as quickly as the majority has built a celebrity up, they can knock them back down.

Enter "cancel culture."

In 2014, a twenty-two-year-old woman named Diamond Strawberry left her daughter, Mylisa, in her own mother's care as she took a chance on love and reality TV stardom.

Diamond moved across the country for a man—Cisco Rosado. Cisco put her up in an apartment (with a room-mate, who he may have also been dating) and the two began

———

68   Dickinson, "Fame is a Fickle Food," Accessed June 14, 2020

to date for the cameras while filming VH1's *Love and Hip Hop: New York.*

Here's all you need to know—Diamond doesn't know where Cisco lives and Cisco doesn't know that Diamond has a six-year old daughter. It's not the most open and honest relationship.

Diamond is out in New York for a short amount of time, has no job or income of note, no real plan for bringing Mylisa out to New York to live with her and is somewhat concerned that Cisco may not be all-in on their relationship.

The two go out to a lunch al-fresco on the Upper West Side and sit down to talk about their current situation. Cisco wears his finest crew neck tee shirt and Diamond wears a skintight dress and heels, because: lunchtime. And almost instantly, the two start to hash out the deep, perplexing aspects of their relationship.[69]

Diamond asks Cisco why she doesn't know where he lives and notes that she is tired of sleeping with him in his car. Cisco claims that he is not ready to make a big commitment to his relationship with Diamond. You know, the kind of commitment where your significant other knows where you live. Big step.

Now, a logical mind might question, "Hmm, shouldn't he have thought about his willingness to commit before making

---

69 Love and Hip Hop: New York, Season 5, Episode 2, "You're Cancelled," December 22, 2014

her move across the country to be with him?" And, perhaps Diamond thinks the same, because in this moment, she determines that she is going to come clean to Cisco that she has a daughter.

This is when things get really good.

Cisco is outraged that Diamond would keep something like a child from him. He cites his "trust issues," which Diamond supposedly knew about and doesn't understand why she would keep this secret from him in their very serious relationship that primarily exists in the back seat of his car.

Cisco shouts, "I just told you I can't trust people and you're going to tell me some bullsh*t that you have a f***ing kid that I don't know about? What's wrong with you?"[70]

Then, Diamond stands up at the table—a bit prematurely for this action to make any real sense—and leans forward to get into Cisco's face. Cisco takes a sip through a straw in his drink, which he then realizes is empty, but still continues to slurp. Diamond and says, "I'm not joking, I'm serious. I have a six-year-old daughter, named Mylisa and I want you to meet her and we're all going to be one big happy family."[71]

Cisco responds (honestly, appropriately), "Are you out of your f***ing mind? Do you hear yourself?"[72]

---

70 Ibid.
71 Ibid.
72 Ibid.

Then, when Diamond suggests that she has not lied to Cisco, she has simply withheld information, Cisco says, "Yo, do me a favor. Get the f**k away from me."[73]

Diamond: "I'm not going no-f**king-where. I came all the way out here to be with you. I'm not going nowhere."[74]

Cisco: "Get the f*ck away from me. You're cancelled."[75]

And so, social media shorthand for anything that is "over" is born.

Cancelled then gains a new definition in Urban Dictionary and is now used to discuss anyone or any idea that has been "culturally blocked from having a prominent public platform or career."[76]

The rise of "cancel culture" and the idea of canceling someone have become polarizing topics of debate as a familiar pattern has emerged: A celebrity or other public figure does or says something offensive. A public backlash, often fueled by politically progressive social media, ensues. Then come the calls to cancel the person—that is, to effectively end their career or revoke their cultural cachet—whether through boycotts of their work or disciplinary action from an employer."[77]

---

73 Ibid.
74 Ibid.
75 Ibid.
76 Romano, "Can't Stop Fighting About Cancel Culture," December 30, 2019.
77 Ibid.

We can't give Cisco Rosado full credit for inciting a cultural phenomenon, however. The idea of cancel culture started with a quote from a 1991 film *New Jack City*, in which Wesley Snipes plays a gangster named Nino Brown. In one scene, after his girlfriend breaks down because of all the violence he's causing, he dumps her by saying, "Cancel that bitch. I'll buy another one."[78]

In 2010, rapper Lil Wayne referenced the line from the film in his song "I'm Single" when he says: "Yeah, I'm single / n***a had to cancel that bitch like Nino."[79] This lyric kept the phrase fresh for the December 2014 use in *Love and Hip Hop*, which gave the concept the wide-reaching platform it truly needed to take off.

After the episode aired, black communities on Twitter— referred to widely as Black Twitter—began using the term "cancelled" in reaction to someone doing something worthy of disapproval, either jokingly or seriously. But, as the term caught on, it quickly began to adopt a specific purpose in the public lexicon. It was a reaction to celebrities when they did something, said something, or shared something that offended.

The media often conflated cancel culture with "outrage culture," but doing so ignores the roots of the phenomenon.

"While the terminology of cancel culture may be new and most applicable to social media through Black Twitter, in

---

78   Ibid.
79   Ibid.

particular, the concept of being canceled is not new to black culture," Anne Charity Hudley, the chair of linguistics of African America for the University of California Santa Barbara, told *Vox*. Hudley, who studies Black vernacular and the use of language in cultural conversations like this one, described canceling as "a survival skill as old as the Southern black use of the boycott."[80]

It invokes the political participation model that if you cannot change something directly, you can protest it and refuse to participate in the objectionable behavior.

"Canceling is a way to acknowledge that you don't have to have the power to change structural inequality," Charity Hudley said. "You don't even have to have the power to change all of public sentiment. But as an individual, you can still have power beyond measure...it's a collective way of saying, 'We elevated your social status, your economic prowess, [and] we're not going to pay attention to you in the way that we once did...I may have no power, but the power I have is to [ignore] you.'"[81]

Cancel culture, in a way, highlights the paradox in our collective obsession with celebrity—be they local relative celebrities or those who attend the red-carpet premieres we watch on network TV.

As I mentioned earlier, America is a nation that prides itself on its citizens' ability to take control of their own

---

80 Ibid.
81 Ibid.

circumstances and manifest their own destiny. We celebrate social and economic mobility in the support of a democratic celebrity, but we see the dark counterpoint of such mobility in cancel culture, where we collectively determine that we can no longer support a celebrity democratically-made.

Think back to the early American experience. For reference, we can look to one of the most in-depth reports of the early American spirit and society, which comes—surprisingly—from a Frenchman who visited the new country to analyze a new form of democracy.

Born in Paris on July 29, 1805, Alexis Charles Henri Clérel de Tocqueville was a member of the French petite noblesse—a nobleman, albeit not the highest ranking. While he traveled throughout the early American continent to observe daily life, he chronicled observations into a book he ultimately published, which—in many ways—charted some profoundly accurate predictions for America's future.

One such prediction that de Tocqueville shared was that anti-aristocratic tendencies of early Americans would grow like seeds, taking root in their minds and spreading to a point where Americans would instinctively come to reject all "forms."[82]

A form, as de Tocqueville would describe it, refers to any manufactured structure in society. Religion is a form. Political association. Gender. Class. Rank.

---

82   De Tocqueville, "Democracy in America," Page 5.

In a conversation I had with Patrick Deneen, a professor of political science at the University of Notre Dame, he explained that de Tocqueville discussed forms as "one of the hallmarks of an aristocratic time." He elaborated: "The aristocratic society was built around rank and inequality of birth and distinctions that are the result of who you are, where you come from, who you come from. These all represent the centrality of forms...So, forms, you could say, became ways that we marked distinctions, as a broad definition."

He continued to explain that we are surrounded by arbitrary forms within society, culture, and politics and de Tocqueville suspected these forms would become objectionable to members of a democratic society.

And this, de Tocqueville suggested, would lead to a society that further scorned forms and formality in almost every aspect of life. Ever called your friends' parents by their first names? Rejection of formality. What about identifying yourself as "spiritual, but not religious." Rejection of formality.

If we expand de Tocqueville's prediction further than he did, having experienced the norms of early American culture, it is easy to see how our rejection of forms has come to bear in modern society. Over the past decade there has been substantial drop-off in identification with organized religion. Today, the role of the community center and local government is dramatically smaller than it was a few decades back. And, broadly, we have come to understand that gender and sexual orientation as a spectrum, instead of a rigid binary state.

As Deenen explained to me, in many ways de Tocqueville was right to predict that we would begin to consider formalized forms highly arbitrary. "This is certainly true of distinctions of classes of people," Deneen shared. "So race would obviously be one, sex, gender would certainly be one—and that's a form that is coming under direct critique and attack in society as being arbitrary."

This is likely driven by the "liberalism" (small "l") that drives much of our American spirit. Our value system fosters the expansion of the liberal the political doctrine that de Tocqueville described as that intended to protect the rights of the individual before the law. But, in his assessment of American culture, and underpinning his predictions for the country and society, de Tocqueville incorporated a healthy dose of skepticism for what this liberal democratic environment would foster. There are certainly qualities in our psychology swim against liberal desires. And de Tocqueville had seen those psychological tendencies play out for the worst.

The man came to America fresh off the French Revolution. His parents were jailed and his grandfather, the Marquis de Rosambo, was sent to the guillotine. Having seen the results of a campaign for "Liberty, Equality and Fraternity," he was, unsurprisingly, skeptical of the justice that would result from majority rule by the people.

However, despite his aristocratic heritage and negative experience with popular rule, de Tocqueville remained sympathetic to American democratic ideals, in particular the "lively instinct for fairness and justice."[83] He ultimately suggested that American democracy would inevitably progress as the "spirit of his age tended increasingly toward more equal and democratic conditions and institutions."[84]

And so, I can't help but feel he would be disappointed in us. We continually allow our natural inclinations to uphold distinctions between societies get the better of us.

"We're really ambivalent about [creating status]," Deneen suggests. "It represents a kind of shadow aristocracy." We have a driving instinct among society—even on the global scale—to ascribe statutes and influential credibility to our peers. And it is in this context that we should consider our relationships with democratic celebrities.

To put Deneen into conversation with Elizabeth Currid-Halkett (a fireside chat I would certainly attend), our ambivalence in awarding status and elevating our peers—influencers and the famous for being famous—to the aristocracy of celebrity has upended the Hollywood ecosystem we once looked to for guidance on who we should admire.

Currid-Halkett wrote in her book, "Gone are the days of the Hollywood studio system and well-oiled PR departments, where actresses were under strict contract to give interviews only to a very select group of media outlets and

---

83   Ibid.
84   Ibid.

those outlets' output was tightly controlled. In the old world of celebrity stars were rarely reported doing anything second to perfection."[85]

We were only permitted to see our celebrities all dolled-up on red carpets. But now, headlines like "Stars, they're just like us!" highlight the pages of every major tabloid. We crave the "tawdry and dull stuff of human existence."[86]

New media, technologies, social platforms, and reality television programming have perpetuated all forms of celebrity, and—in turn—have reduced barriers to entry unlike any other point in history. To be admired by the masses is our modern-day Beouwolfian (yup, went there) virtue. The influencer economy is fueled by a tidal wave of people attempting to demonstrate that they are not only keenest to win fame, but also worthiest of that fame. Or, as Currid-Halkett wrote, "the feeling that people without experience, expert knowledge, skill, learning or aptitude had something extra, something special to offer" would come to replace the talent-led industry of celebrity we once recognized as the Hollywood Elite.[87]

It will continually gain fuel from our cultural desire to believe that we, too, could achieve some level of super-stardom. It's our appreciation and support that has made these democratic celebrities just as legitimate as their talented peers.

---

85 Currid-Halkett, "Starstruck," Kindle Location 186.
86 Ibid.
87 Ibid.

THE CELEBRITY SCAPEGOAT

I am writing this book amid a global pandemic. COVID-19 has upended every aspect of our lives, creating situations that require us to rethink the ways that we live, work, and interact, and for influencers and content creators it has created some problems.

These people have amassed impressive wealth stemming from near-constant self-promotion and product endorsement. Their self-centered attitudes and luxurious lifestyles made them famous in the first place. But amid headlines of one-hundred thousand American deaths, skyrocketing unemployment, and resulting economic distress, resentment of privilege is rising.

Arielle Charnas, a fashion blogger turned Instagram influencer and head of the clothing brand Something Navy (named after her blog), was among the first in the pandemic to experience the wrath of an audience offended by how much their day-to-day no longer felt relatable to this influencer's experience.

Charnas used her own personal connections with a doctor to get access to a COVID-19 test—at the time incredibly hard to come by—because she was feeling ill. She took her followers on the journey with her and many questioned whether her seemingly mild symptoms warranted her leaving her home and taking a test away from someone who may potentially be more at risk. Later, Charnas posted that she had—in fact—tested positive for COVID-19.

As Charnas tested positive, she and her husband, their two children—and their nanny—decided to leave the epicenter of the US outbreak, New York City, and head to their second home in the Hamptons, where the family would have more space. This was Charnas' second major mistake. Most of the population had been following strict shelter-in-place orders across the country and were starting to wonder if we would ever be allowed out of the house again. That's when Charnas packed up her family, hopped in the car, and took her germs to the Hamptons, where she started posting photos of herself in tie-dye sweat suits cuddling her daughters, in close proximity to her husband and nanny, and also modeling her outfits from the porch of the enormous home.

This, while many parents around the country were trying to manage work-from-home situations with no childcare, remote schooling for their children, all while worrying that their loved ones could catch a virus that might take their lives.

Charnas' charmed life felt offensive to many in the face of such a serious global issue. People pushed back. Charnas was one of the first celebrities in the pandemic to be cancelled. Her "authentic" persona no longer seemed relatable and, as a result, her audience—those who enabled her major economic successes in the first place—no longer saw their own experiences reflected through Charnas' Instagram-filtered lens, and therefore took offense to her flaunting her fortune and privilege. People started to boycott her brand.

A FINE BALANCE

Where Charnas failed, many others have succeeded. There is a certain level of awareness required to maintain a brand on social media that shamelessly markets oneself, all while feeling authentic and unapologetic. And no one walks this line better than Kim K.

Kardashian was an early adopter of social media (specifically Twitter) and uses the tools and access to her base of followers to create the persona she wants others to see. She builds her credibility in two ways: 1) Reassuring fans of her normality and likable nature and 2) spotlighting her glamorous lifestyle and celebrity acquaintances.[88]

This may seem divergent. It is. But it's effective.

In *Keeping Up the Kardashian Brand*, author Amanda Scheiner McClain analyzed a year of Kim's Twitter activity and broke her engagements out into a handful of categories.

"Kim's Twitter exemplifies the new face of celebrity," said McClain. "By actively embracing social media to detail the minutia of her life, Kim constructs a persona with a number of dualities: ordinary / extraordinary, likable / famous, authentic / glamorous."[89] This research focused on Twitter, but Kim embraces a similar structure on her Instagram page as well.

On these platforms, Kardashian curates the content that she shares to show her followers that she is thinking about them throughout the day. She details her dedication to her role in the public eye by giving viewers a view into her 5 a.m. gym sessions to tone her iconic figure, she gets candid about the

---

88 McClain, "Keeping up the Kardashian Brand," Page 85.
89 McClain, "Keeping up the Kardashian Brand," Page 85.

burn out of a life on the road and days packed with public engagements, she showcases downtime with her family— whether watching *Family Feud* with Kanye or playing dress up with North—and throughout it all, she highlights her many brands and product endeavors.

McClain breaks out Kim's engagements into four classifications of social media post:[90]

- **Personal Tidbits**: These anecdotes we might not get from a traditional interview give fans a sense of the "real Kim" and build her credibility and authenticity. These updates could be as simple as "I'm addicted to french fries. #help." But they make Kim feel relatable and approachable.
- **Fan Interactions:** Kim learned early on that Twitter could be one of the best focus groups she'd ever have access to. In the spirit of maintaining that level of engagement, Kim regularly directly interacts with her fans and followers, answering questions or dispelling rumors. She regularly thanks her followers for the role that they have played in enabling her success, and credits them as much as her own hard work for all she has achieved. These posts make Kim appear grateful and aware that she could lose her democratic celebrity should the populace that promoted her to status lose interest. Finally, she regularly polls her followers for ideas and suggestions for everything from new music she should download to new skincare products she should try for her psoriasis. These calls for input make Kim feel very ordinary and easy to relate to. She looks to advice from us, the same way we look to her.

---

90 McClain, "Keeping up the Kardashian Brand," Pages 75-85.

- **Lifestyle Updates:** These posts give audiences a look at what it takes to maintain Kim's fabulous life. "Rise and Grind" is a frequent morning post letting her fans know that she is awake and working. "I can't believe it's 4:30 AM and I'm up for a full press day! #sleepy" demonstrates her commitment to showing up for her fans. They showcase how famous Kim really is and shine a light on her busy schedule, but they also promote the perception that she has earned this celebrity and works for it every day.

- **Celebrity interactions:** Last, and most importantly, Kim showcases the elite social ecosystem of which she is central. She posts pictures with fellow celebrities. She tags other celebrities she ran into at parties or social outings. She shines a light on the exclusivity of her ecosystem and, in doing so, makes herself appear more elusive and worthy of adoration. It's the most fundamental of celebrity-building tactics—see and be seen.

And we all follow along, on the edge of our seats. We anxiously await posts giving us a glimpse her busy and exotic life. Her candid disclosures knit the fabric of our remote friendships with her. Her acknowledgement that she is thinking of us—the followers—over social media by asking our opinions in polls or calling for comments on a post make us feel valued. And her lifestyle updates, complete with a birds-eye view of into her exclusive social circle, excessively programmed events—like children's birthday parties that likely cost more than most people's wedding days—and general luxury experiences make us pointedly aware that she is not at all "just like us."

AMERICAN INDIVIDUALISM GONE AWRY?

I believe that de Tocqueville was an early prophet for American influencer culture. He saw the roots of this social phenomena in his tour of America in the 1800s, and he warned of the potential impact of materialism and individualism on the nation. I don't think he could have ever imagined the scale of this trend enabled by social media, but we can forgive him this short-sighted assessment; he could never have fathomed the communications technologies we have available today.

In fact, it is in de Tocqueville's time that we first encounter a term that will come to define modern society: individualism. De Tocqueville writes that "individualism is of democratic origin and it threatens to spread in the same ration as the equality of condition."[91]

American individualism, which is defined as a theory favoring freedom of action for individuals and self-reliance over collective control, follows naturally from the liberal doctrine that molded the founding view of the American system. It is frequently coupled with terms like egalitarianism, and exalted as a fundamental, revolutionary American ideal. But the word "individualism" didn't even appear in the English language until 1839, more than fifty years *after* the American Revolution.[92]

There is no doubt that the rights of the individual were top-of-mind for the American founding fathers. Their legacy permeates our understanding of the country to this day, with

---

91   De Tocqueville, "Democracy in America," Page 5.
92   Grabb, Baer and Curtis, "Origins of American Individualism," Pages 511-533.

school children pledging allegiance to a flag that represents liberty and justice for all. But our current understanding of individualism—self-expression by monologues delivered via Instagram stories and YouTube videos, the mobilizing rallying cry, "Imma do me, you can do you"—are likely not what Patrick Henry imagined for this nation when he proclaimed, "Give me liberty, or give me death."

For the Founding Fathers, it was religious and economic freedoms that inspired their support for liberty and limited government, protecting the rights of the individual and preaching: "A wise and frugal government…shall restrain men from injuring one another, shall leave them otherwise free to regulate their own pursuits of industry and improvement, and shall not take from the mouth of labor the bread it has earned. This is the sum of good government."[93]

We are taught to value American individualism early in life.

When I was in kindergarten, every member of my class was instructed to stand in front of our class and proclaim that they were unique:

"My name is Clare Carluccio, and I am unique."

But one could argue that this recognition of the individual and encouragement to chart one's own path apart from the community risks an over-rotation toward valuing self-importance in place of civic virtue. We start to put the good of the

---

93 Jefferson, "First Inaugural Address," March 4, 1801.

self ahead of the good of the community. And we certainly see that play out in the celebrities we've rewarded over time.

Like so many of his reflections, de Tocqueville was eerily accurate in his prediction for the spread of individualist spirit in America. He cautioned that the result of this value will be to dispose "each member of the community to sever himself from the mass of his fellows, and to draw apart with his family and his friends; so that, after he has thus formed a little circle of his own, he willingly leaves society at large to itself."[94] Continuing that beyond the short term withdrawal from civic life, individualism risked destroying interpersonal relationships, as it ultimately leads people to become "absorbed in downright selfishness."[95]

So, instead of Benjamin Franklin's reflection that "It is the first responsibility of every citizen to question authority," we get, "So, a lot of you have asked me about my skincare routine..."

---

94 Tocqueville, "Democracy in America," Page 223.
95 Ibid.

5

ACHIEVING THE NEW AMERICAN DREAM

———

With so many influencers in the world, what separates the successful from the unsuccessful? And who is even paying attention to all these people?

I am.

It's time for my second confession. I am a social media stalker. I am not a huge social media participant. I almost exclusively use Instagram, and even there, I post infrequently. But I can uncover a huge amount of information by doing quick scans of the feeds on my social media platforms.

I'll come home from work, switch into some cozy clothes, pour myself a glass of wine, and put my feet up while I open up Instagram and start to scroll. Then I start texting a variety of friends:

"You know, Mary hasn't posted a photo with her fiancé for quite some time; I wonder if they've postponed the wedding."

"Oh wow. Julie paid Ryan and included the pizza emoji on Venmo. Things must be getting serious if she's paying for dinner."

"Oh! Patrick is on vacation the same spot I'm heading in a few days. I should reach out!...Okay, you're right. There is no chance I will reach out. I'll simply pretend to be surprised when I run into him."

It's a gift. It also highlights just how pervasive (and invasive) social media can really be. But use of a wide-reaching platform is not all it takes to build influence.

THE AMERICAN DREAM

As schoolchildren, we are introduced to the concept of the American Dream in an early stage history class. My first introduction of the term came shortly after the conclusion of a School House Rock video where a cartoon sang to me about how there would be "Fireworks on the Fourth of July. Red, white, and blue fireworks, like diamonds in the sky."[96]

Our teacher had wheeled in the boxy television that sat atop that rolling cart covered in extension cords and Velcro that no one ever really touched or needed. Now, that TV was usually reserved for student entertainment when the teacher was out sick and hadn't left detailed lesson plans for the substitute teacher, so you can imagine our excitement when the TV rolled in during regularly scheduled history class.

---

96 Ahrens, "Fireworks," 1977.

The teacher passed out the lyrics to the song and told us to follow along with the movie.

The Declaration of Independence. / Oh yeah! /
In seventeen hundred seventy six. / Right on!/
The Continental Congress said that we were free./
Said we had the right to life and liberty/
(spoken) And the pursuit of happiness.[97]

And when the clip finished, she switched off the TV and asked my class, "What does this mean to you?"

Crickets. The class just looked up at her. We had never heard most of these words before and therefore, it didn't mean anything to us.

And so my teacher jumped back in to explain (I paraphrase):

This is the promise that our Founding Fathers made to each other and to all of the early settlers in America. That we would always have the freedom to try and improve our livelihoods and the lives of those around us. When they talk about the pursuit of happiness, that is the promise that they are making to all of us. That every person who lives in this country will be able to choose their own path, and will always have the freedom to pursue whatever they want. This is what is known as the American Dream.

From this very early introduction to the concept of the American Dream, we are taught the value of hard work and merit. It is a deeply rooted seed that drives us to want to improve

---

97   Ibid.

our status; it's planted in our minds as part of our uniquely American idealism.

The idea of the American Dream was first introduced by James Truslow Adams in his 1931 book titled *The Epic of America*. His definition of the dream is "that dream of a land in which life should be better and richer and fuller for everyone, with opportunity for each according to ability or achievement...It is not a dream of motor cars and high wages merely, but a dream of social order in which each man and each woman shall be able to attain to the fullest stature of which they are innately capable, and be recognized by others for what they are, regardless of the fortuitous circumstances of birth or position."[98]

The dream has taken on many interpretations over the course of American history. From the dream of settling new land and exploring the American frontier, to the luck and discovery that led to the Gold Rush fortunes. But the dream—at least as we receive it early on in childhood—is always framed to us as something that can be achieved. You just need to go after it.

The success of the American Dream is reinforced later in our education as we read quotes from Martin Luther King's letter from Birmingham Jail, in which he equates the protests of Black Americans who participated in sit-ins and marches to actions that should be recognized as "standing up for the American dream...thereby bringing our nation back to those great wells of democracy which were dug deep by the

---

98   Adams, *The Epic of America*, 1931.

Founding Fathers in their formulation of the Constitution and the Declaration of Independence."[99]

As we are taught about the American Dream, we learn about a certain level of "bootstrapping" required for its fulfillment. To truly be a self-made success, there will be times of hardship that you must overcome. We need to understand your journey as that of a narrative hero. We need to *see* your struggles to ensure you're worthy of our praise.

In a content-rich environment, the role in influencer extends beyond that of a mere content creator. To truly influence audiences and assume the role of the democratic celebrity, an influencer needs to foster deeper relationships with followers. Otherwise, people like me, sitting on my couch and scrolling after work, will begin to classify your content as "fake."

I'll explain exactly what I mean using an example from my own hometown. I find any chance I can to talk about this one person from my high school who has a truly perplexing social media presence, and so, I thought, "What better place to immortalize his influencer aspirations than in a book?"

You see, around the time that I was graduating high school, Facebook came onto the scene. As a result, I have a lot of high school Facebook friends, many of whom I never spoke to in school, and most of whom I have no interest in keeping tabs on. That is, except for one guy. I will change his name for privacy purposes. Let's call him Steve Stevens.

---

99   King Jr., "Letter from a Birmingham Jail," April 16, 1963.

Now, Steve was an average guy during our high school days. He played soccer and seemed to have a fair amount of friends. He was neither crazy popular, nor unpopular. But, about two years after college (again, never having spoken to Steve and still not intending to speak to him), my friends and I realized that he had changed his name to (again, altered for privacy) Mike Michaels on all forms of social media. What's important to understand here is that he went from one totally average name to another totally average name, but with this name change came a bit of a personality shift.

Suddenly, Mike Michaels was updating his thousands of followers on Facebook with his opinions of the world. At all times. He shared everything from bragging about his new job in finance to rants about never listening to the radio in the car because of the deteriorating state of pop music.

My friends regularly share updates of encounters with the Facebook legend Mike Michaels. Run-ins at the train station, sightings from around Midtown Manhattan, and most importantly—truly unbelievable status updates shared across social media that help get us all through the 3 p.m. workday slump:

"You can't soar like an eagle if you hang out with chickens."

"The best part of Mother's Day is getting to see who has hot moms on Facebook."

"I netted $17 million for my company in April...what did you do?"

Nevertheless, his reach doesn't seem to extend beyond those who know him in some capacity, despite a concerted effort to do so. And I doubt that anyone is taking his opinions into account when shaping their own world views. I certainly won't allow his distaste for pop music stop me from pre-ordering the next Taylor Swift album and, if anything, reading his posts makes me resent his apparent success at his job and question if he really did net that $17 million for his company in April.

It's unlikely that he did. And he certainly didn't do it alone.

In fact, Mike Michaels is, in many ways, a cautionary tale of what can become of the social media influencer if content strays too far outside of the relatable. The veneer he applies to his (likely) mundane life in finance quickly becomes fuel for mockery.

As content has grown more abundant, internet culture has made us recognize success under the umbrella of a pre-defined set of rules.

Founder of influencer marketing agency Viral Nation, Joe Gagliese, shared in an interview with NPR that many of the influencers we see in our feed are ascribing to the Instagram aesthetic—a highly-designed, artfully edited version of reality. The aesthetic was born of early influencers, taking inspiration from the glossy-paged professional photography we see in traditional magazines.[100]

---

100 Sanders, "The New Celebrity," September 10, 2019.

However, the aesthetic sparked a trend where full experiences designed exclusively to be photographed and shared on social media began popping up around the country. The Museum of Ice Cream. The Rose Mansion. The graffiti-inspired, brightly patterned "Instagram Wall." Even full restaurants designed to be photographed—for example the all-Millennial Pink painted restaurant Pietro Nolita in New York City, which is, apart from its color, exactly what you would expect of a restaurant near Little Italy.

These often for-purchase experiences are designed to provide the amateur Instagrammer the ability to snap a quick photo with their own cell phone camera and achieve the same level of professional editing and detail that the early influencers chased.

Mike Michaels' social media veneer was his own odd version of the Instagram aesthetic. He saw other influencers shamelessly promoting their wealth and success and assumed that level of haughty attention-seeking would translate for him as well. But it never quite struck the right chord, and that is largely because he was making his play for influencer stardom in 2019, when established influencers and democratic celebrities alike began backing away from the overly polished Instagram aesthetic.

Embodying this trend is a wave of memes focused on illustrating "Instagram vs. Reality." These memes started as a way for people to remind the social media universe not to believe everything they see on social media. They feature side-by-sides of images providing audiences a wider lens to the content they consume throughout the day from influencers. For example, that perfect photo of an aspiring model perfectly made up, clad in a boho-chic outfit and laying in a field surrounded by brightly colored flowers and then contrast it to a wider view of the scene where the image was shot. The grass is mostly dead, the flowers have been planted around the model. It's clear that the image was entirely manufactured.

We're already seeing shifts in influencer content fueled by the "Instagram vs. Reality" movement.

In an article for *The Atlantic* discussing the abrupt abandonment of the Instagram aesthetic, Taylor Lorenz reported that in 2019 at Beautycon, a beauty product trade show, "Instagram stars spoke about moving away from ring lights and toward showing off their faces in sunlight. As the public becomes more aware of the prevalence of sponsored posts, beauty influencers are abandoning branded shots for ones that show off their 'empties' (empty bottles of product they actually use)."[101]

Lorenz interviewed a fifteen-year-old girl, because obviously we're seeking insights for future of social media marketing from the only people who innately understand social media— teenagers—who stated of the aesthetic: "You can photoshop any girl into that background and it will be the same post... It's not cool anymore to be manufactured."[102]

Another influencer interviewed for the article stated: "For my generation, people are more willing to be who they are

---

101 Lorenz, "The Instagram Aesthetic is Over," April 23, 2019.
102 Ibid.

and not make up a fake identity...We are trying to show a real person doing cool things as a real person, not trying to create a persona that isn't actually you."[103]

The Instagram aesthetic is, for them, as undesirable as a photo taken without a well-executed "skinny arm" would be to some of their predecessors.

And there is a lot of success to be had—if you can effectively break out of the aesthetic.

Gagliese notes that there's a really big distinction between the level of influence you can have ascribing to the Instagram aesthetic and "true influence."[104]

"You don't want to be an influencer that people just look at," Gagliese said.[105] "You want to be someone who can give a recommendation to their audience, and they're interested in what your recommendation is and may act on that recommendation."[106] The first influencer who undoubtedly achieved the level of influence where she can give a recommendation and her audience would likely act on it showed us exactly how big an economic asset social media and personal brand can be. She comes from social media's royal family— the Kardashians—and in 2019 she was reported to be the world's youngest self-made billionaire.

Her name is Kylie Jenner.

—————————————

103 Ibid.
104 Sanders, "The New Celebrity," September 10, 2019.
105 Ibid.
106 Ibid.

WHAT IT MEANS TO BE SELF-MADE

For about a decade, nearly all focus among the Kardashian family was trained on Kim, Khloe, and Kourtney, but recently the leading driver of Kardashian Konversation is the youngest member of the family: Kylie. In 2019, *Forbes* reported that at twenty-one, Jenner was on track to become the youngest self-made billionaire ever, an achievement made possible—in large part—by her ability to build an empire on top of a rock-solid foundation of social media followers.[107]

In the *Forbes* profile of Jenner, she herself credits her social media platforms for her accelerated success.

"It's the power of social media," Jenner says. "I had such a strong reach before I was able to start anything."[108] She uses her presence on social media to announce new makeup shades and skincare products, as well as previewing new items on herself and—in doing so—acts as her own personal brand endorsement, making a trustworthy recommendation directly to her 160+ million followers.

Think about it. Jenner was a teen for the dawn of social media. She has lived her life in the spotlight, as a result of her older sibling's participation in *Keeping Up With the Kardashians*, so in many ways she was groomed for influencer life beginning at ten years old.

As a digital and social media native, Jenner understood inherently how her peers and broader audience were using

---

107 Robehmed, "At 21, Kylie Jenner Becomes The Youngest Self-Made Billionaire Ever," March 5, 2019.
108 Ibid.

social media. She was one of the first celebrities, and arguably the most successful, to adopt Snapchat stories as a means of direct-to-fan communication.

Through her social media presence, fans got to see a side of Jenner that wasn't made available to the masses on *Keeping Up*. Her personality started to ring through in a way that the editors often didn't feature on E! She was able to differentiate herself from her sisters and showed that she was ready to claim her rightful place in democratic celebrity stardom. Her explosion onto the social media scene even helped her secure a spin off reality show production—separate from *Keeping Up—Life of Kylie*.

All the while, Jenner's physical image was shifting. She started to dress more like her older sisters. She was highlighting the famous Kardashian curves and, most controversially, started enhancing the size of her lips.

The public, having seen footage of Kylie for a decade, was quick to accuse her of plastic surgery or other alterations. There was outrage that someone so young—she was just seventeen at the time—would be going under the knife before her body had even fully developed.

But, through all the accusations, Jenner maintained that she had not had any procedures done to alter her appearance. Her lips were merely full and plump because she was using new makeup techniques that involved "overlining" her lips to make them appear larger. She even regularly shared tutorials of how she over lined her lips, highlighting her Kylie Cosmetics products throughout, and raked in the profits from booming sales of her lip kits.

However—knowing all that we know now about the desire for candid interactions between fans and celebrities on social media—ultimately Jenner's followers (and many in the broader media and commentary ecosystem) pushed back against her explanations. I'll bet they tried overlining their lips and received less-than-desirable results. Many started criticizing Jenner for her lack of transparency.

Assessing the public relations issue at hand, Jenner decided in 2017 to come clean with her audience in a confessional-style interview on *Keeping Up With the Kardashians*.[109] She additionally shared a post across her platforms disclosing that she had—in fact—been receiving injections to increase the size of her lips.

In the confessional, Jenner opened up about a formative experience from her early teenage years during which a boy she had a crush on had told her she had really small lips and, as a result, probably wasn't going to be a good kisser. Prior to this interaction, Jenner shared that she had many insecurities about her appearance—as nearly all teenagers do—but this interaction solidified her shortcomings in her own mind.

In her own words, "I took that really hard...I don't know, it just really affected me. I just didn't feel desirable or pretty. I really wanted bigger lips...It just sticks with you."[110]

For most of Jenner's audience, this rationale hit home. It is very natural to have insecurities about one's own appearance,

---

109 *Keeping Up With the Kardashians*, Season 10, Episode 9,"Lip Service," May 10, 2015.
110 Ibid.

particularly if it has been a point of criticism by any jerk in the past, and so upon hearing her rationale, Jenner's fans rushed to support her.

Jenner received credit for her unfiltered, raw, and real interactions. She basically had her own "I chopped down the cherry tree" moment and, just like our first President, was lauded for her honesty and transparency.

And that trust and transparency furthered her brand and her economic interests. Today, Kylie Jenner is believed to be worth nearly $1 billion dollars, and her influence is expanding every day.

When Kylie achieved the recognition from *Forbes* as the world's youngest self-made billionaire, public backlash surged. Audiences questioned how we could possibly consider Jenner a self-made woman. Memes circulated poking fun at Jenner's early mornings running her paper route to save up for her first big investments. But, at the end of the day, Jenner did earn her fortune.

From her very young appearances on *Keeping Up With the Kardashians*, Jenner saved her wages, and as hype around her and Kendall grew, the two began expanding their public appearances and modeling opportunities.

When she came up with the idea for the Lip Kit in 2015, she took money from her own lifetime of unorthodox earnings and placed a bet on a venture that could have gone south, launching at small scale to test the market for her product.

The trio of lipsticks she debuted sold out instantly.

She then leveraged her network of influential siblings to grow her product portfolio, made ventures into brick and mortar retail with targeted pop up shops, and explored retail partnerships with global brands like Topshop, all while maintaining incredibly low overhead costs for production and a 90 percent stake ownership in Kylie Cosmetics.[111]

In 2019, Kylie partnered with Ulta Beauty for an exclusive distribution deal that enabled her to further scale her business and take her seven-person team and cult following into the big leagues, disrupting storied brands like Revlon and L'Oréal. Later that year, Kylie sold a majority stake in her company to Coty beauty for $600 million.[112]

In our new world order, Kylie Jenner *is* the American Dream. Or at least, she was.

---

111 Robehmed, "At 21, Kylie Jenner Becomes The Youngest Self-Made Billionaire Ever," March 5, 2019.
112 Ibid.

6

CREDIBILITY AND NEW MEDIA

———

"Inside Kylie Jenner's Web of Lies, and Why She's No Longer a Billionaire," reads the May 29, 2020 headline in *Forbes*—the very publication that first gave her a credible claim to the billionaire title.[113] The article sent shock waves through the pop culture ecosystem.

"What am I even waking up to. I thought this was a reputable site...all i see are a number of inaccurate statements and unproved assumptions lol. I've never asked for any title or tried to lie my way there EVER. period," tweeted Kylie in response to the article.[114]

The article alleges that the Kylie Jenner Billionaires Issue cover story was the result of an extensive public relations campaign, on behalf of Kylie, to prove her net worth to the

———

113 Peterson-Withorn and Berg, "Kylie Jenner's Web of Lies," May 29, 2020.
114 Kylie Jenner, Twitter Post, May 29, 2020.

business publication. But, following the sale of Kylie Cosmetics, "filings released by publicly traded Coty over the past six months lay bare one of the family's best-kept secrets: Kylie's business is significantly smaller, and less profitable, than the family has spent years leading the cosmetics industry and media outlets, including *Forbes*, to believe."[115]

The article continues that in an attempt to secure a cover story celebrating Kylie's net worth, the Kardashian-Jenner team invited *Forbes* reporters to meetings with their accountants and shared tax return documents that the *Forbes* team now alleges were falsified to augment the appearance of Kylie's worth.

If we are to believe the *Forbes* report, Kylie's PR team was actively working to prove that revenues of Kylie Cosmetics were "$400 million over the business' first 18 months...with a personal take-home pay of $250 million for Kylie."[116] But based on *Forbes*' assessment of Kylie's business assets detailed in the Coty filings, "revenues over a 12-month period preceding the deal: $177 million... far lower than the published estimates at the time. More problematic, Coty said that sales were up 40 percent from 2018, meaning the business only generated about $125 million that year, nowhere near the $360 million the Jenners had led *Forbes* to believe."[117]

At the end of the day, *Forbes* still concedes that Jenner is worth $900 million.[118] But the allegations and he-said /

---

115 Peterson-Withorn and Berg, "Kylie Jenner's Web of Lies," May 29, 2020.
116 Ibid.
117 Ibid.
118 Ibid.

she-said nature of the reporting is not what we would traditionally expect from a leading business outlet.

Throughout the article, the *Forbes* reporters note that:

"[*Forbes*] was shown tax returns detailing $307 million in 2016 revenues and personal income of more than $110 million for Kylie that year. It would have been enough to put her at No. 2 on the Celebrity 100 list, behind only Taylor Swift, the accountant was quick to point out. But the documents, despite looking authentic and bearing Kylie Jenner's signature, weren't exactly convincing since the story they told, of e-commerce brand Kylie Cosmetics growing from nothing to $300 million in sales in a single year, was hard to believe."[119]

Now, *Forbes* has long been in the business of tracking, analyzing, and reporting on the wealthiest individuals in the world, and the company has a very analytical approach to determining net worth.

So, it is interesting to hear the reporters note that even after they took the meetings with Kylie's accounting team back in 2017, they were skeptical of the reported growth that the Kardashian-Jenner family was claiming. The reporters note that the *Forbes* team continued vetting the performance metrics of Kylie Cosmetics with industry analysts, many of whom were also of the opinion that the rate of growth seemed too large to be possible.[120]

---

119 Ibid.
120 Ibid.

In the exposé, the *Forbes* team notes that "after speaking with a handful of analysts and industry experts who also found the Jenners' claims implausible, we settled on a more reasonable estimate for our 2017 Celebrity 100 list: $41 million in overall earnings for Kylie, good for the No. 59 spot."[121]

The reporters then suggest that after *Forbes* had rejected the story that the Kardashian-Jenner team was promoting, the PR team that first engaged *Forbes* took the same high-value story to another outlet: *Women's Wear Daily* (*WWD*). It's important to note that *WWD* is known as a highly influential fashion and beauty outlet, but is not, necessarily, known for its in-depth business and finance reporting.

On August 9, 2017, *WWD* reported "Kylie Jenner's Kylie Cosmetics On Way to Becoming $1B Brand," including the stat *Forbes* reports it had rejected in its sub headline: "Kylie Cosmetics has done $420 million in retail sales in just 18 months." [122]

I want to put some of these numbers into context for you all. Tom Ford Beauty, an Estée Lauder Company, is said to be one of the holding company's fastest growing brands and only reached the $500 million revenue mark after more than a *decade* in operation.[123] The *WWD* article further reported that Bobbi Brown, another leading brand under the Estée

121 Ibid.
122 Strugatz, "Kylie Cosmetics On Its Way To Becoming $1B Brand," August 9, 2017.
123 Ibid.

Lauder umbrella, took twenty-five years to reach the billion-dollar threshold.[124]

With that in mind, we can understand why the *Forbes* team was initially skeptical of the impressively large figures the Jenner team was sharing.

But once *WWD* shared this report, the valuation went viral. Business magazine *Fortune* cited the interview and documentation provided to *WWD* as proof that Kylie Cosmetics had pulled in $420 million in retail sales over its first eighteen months, and shared the projections for 2017 that suggested the company was on track to earn $1 billion by 2022.[125] CNBC reported on "How Kylie Jenner turned her $29 lipstick business into a $420 million empire in 18 months."[126] Again, this report exclusively pointed to the *WWD* article as validation of the success of Kylie's business.

Once that number was out there, the "unicorns" of the beauty industry became the talk of the town. The term Unicorn, in this sense, originated as a way to describe Silicon Valley startups that had been valued at $1 billion or more. They were companies like Instagram, Uber, and WeWork. But following Kylie's Unicorn valuation in *WWD*, we started to hear more about a number of female-led beauty brand unicorns popping up around the country—for example, Emily Weiss's makeup brand, Glossier, and Huda Kattan's Huda Beauty. Both—like

---

124 Ibid

125 Zorthian, "Kylie Jenner's Cosmetics Brand Is on Track to Become a $1 Billion Company," August 10, 2017.

126 Mejia, "Kylie Jenner $420 million empire in 18 months," September 14, 2017.

Kylie cosmetics—were valued around $1 billion dollars and followed a direct-to-consumer business model that required very little overhead and management. Further, they leveraged incredibly enthusiastic fan bases on social media to build the brands and create incredible demand.[127]

So, by the time *Forbes* started to assess brand valuations for its 2017 Billionaire's list, analysts weren't nearly as skeptical of the incredibly high valuation of Kylie Cosmetics.

When the *Forbes* team reconnected with the Kardashian-Jenner family, Jenner's team reported that "2017 revenues were up 7 percent, they said, to $330 million. 'No other influencer has ever gotten to the volume or had the rabid fans and consistency that Kylie has had for the last two and a half years,' an executive at e-commerce platform Shopify, which manages Kylie's online store, told *Forbes* at the time."[128]

So, based largely on the numbers disclosed directly by the Kardashian-Jenner family and validation of industry analysts singing a different tune than they did the year before, *Forbes* determined that Kylie Jenner was on track to become the world's youngest self-made billionaire and awarded her the cover story of its 2018 Billionaire's issue.

In the expose on Kylie's financials, *Forbes* reported: "At age twenty, she was worth $900 million, we estimated, and would soon become the youngest self-made billionaire ever."[129] But

---

127 Malle, "Billion Dollar Unicorns Changing Beauty Industry," July 22, 2019.
128 Peterson-Withorn and Berg, "Kylie Jenner's Web of Lies," May 29, 2020.
129 Ibid.

following the sale of her business to Coty, Kylie's financials became a subject of public disclosure, and *Forbes* alleges that the numbers they were led to believe in 2018 would not have been possible based on the numbers disclosed in Coty's public filings.

One of the industry veterans cited in the *Forbes* exposé, Jeffrey Ten—who has led companies including Note Cosmetics, Nyx, and Calvin Klein Beauty—noted that the sale to Coty suggests that it is unlikely that the Kylie Cosmetics business could have cratered so dramatically during the year. If it had, he questions, "why would Coty buy it?"[130]

The *Forbes* report therefore positions this interaction (among others) as evidence that the Kylie Cosmetics team must have been exaggerating their revenue and performance since the very start of the business.

And, as stated by the *Forbes* team following a multi-month investigative report, "virtually every" industry expert consulted "thinks the business couldn't have collapsed by so much so quickly...More likely: The business was never that big to begin with, and the Jenners have lied about it every year since 2016—including having their accountant draft tax returns with false numbers—to help juice *Forbes'* estimates of Kylie's earnings and net worth. While we can't prove those documents were fake (though it's likely), it's clear that Kylie's camp has been lying."[131]

The article then looks back to Jeffrey Ten for further context.

---

130 Ibid.
131 Ibid.

"You have to remember they are in the entertainment business," he stated. "Everything in entertainment has to be exaggerated to get attention."[132]

Jenner was outraged.

"That's your proof? So you just THOUGHT they were forged? like actually what am i reading." the follow-up tweet from Kylie retorted.[133]

And, at the end of the day, I can't blame Jenner for expressing her discontent for the details shared in the article.

In reporting that it is "likely" that the Jenners forged official documents, even based on conversations with industry analysts and assessment of now public filings, is a major accusation and, based on *this* PR professional's read of the article, is not a bulletproof argument.

On June 1, 2020, the *Forbes* article was updated to include a statement from a broader response shared by representatives of Kylie and Kris Jenner, which stated that "the accusations that the Jenners, and/or their accountants, falsified tax returns and then lied about their 2016 revenues for the last four years, are absolutely false."[134]

So, who are we to believe?

---

132 Ibid.
133 Kylie Jenner, Twitter Post, May 20, 2020.
134 Peterson-Withorn and Berg, "Kylie Jenner's Web of Lies," May 29, 2020.

QUESTIONING CREDIBILITY

It's nearly impossible to know who to trust in the Internet Age. In his book, *Influence*, Robert Cialdini talks about some of the psychology behind the human instinct to allow our opinions to be shaped by others.

He writes, "Very often, in making decisions about someone or something, we don't use all the relevant information; we include only a single, highly representative piece of the total. And an isolated piece of information...can lead us to clearly stupid mistakes."[135]

However, I'm not sure how life would progress if we didn't use these shortcuts to make decisions. We would spend our entire lives reading up on all the available information, weighing pros and cons, and trying to approach the objective truth before acting.

In a world where nearly everyone is a publisher, we'll probably never get over the hurdle of asking ourselves where to begin.

In Cialdini's terms: "With the sophisticated mental apparatus we have used to build world eminence as a species, we have created an environment so complex, fast paced, and information-laden that we must increasingly deal with it in the fashion of the animals we so long ago transcended."[136]

---

135 Cialdini, *Influence*, Page 274.
136 Cialdini, *Influence*, 275.

But this presents a problem when our trustworthy sources—
sources like major media brands (ahem *Forbes*) provide con-
flicting counsel and direction.

In the Kylie Jenner Billionaires Issue example, if we are to believe
the *Forbes* retraction, they are admitting to using a shortcut to
establish their own misinformed conclusion that Kylie Jenner
was to be the world's youngest self-made billionaire.

They looked at a trend toward billion-dollar valued beauty
brands, received counsel from some industry analysts, and
concluded that the numbers they themselves once rejected
as unrealistic must have been, in fact, true.

And, as the pace of information creation continues to accelerate, and the ways we receive information continue to evolve,
we've seen our traditionally trustworthy sources of information—the mainstream media—fall victim to more and more
trickery based on clickbait in an increasingly competitive
content landscape.

It is, unfortunately, a critical reality for a lot of the media
brands I work with regularly in my day job. Editorial teams
are shrinking, the pace required to cover breaking news is
accelerating, and overall numbers of subscribers are drop-
ping by the day. And a lot of it is driven by the near-instan-
taneous nature of information sharing on social media.

ALL THE NEWS THAT'S FIT TO SHARE

At the Design Center in San Francisco on April 10, 2010,
attendees can tell that something big is about to happen.

A massive screen projects blue animations over the crowd; reporters from major start-up media like TechCrunch, live bloggers, and other members of the Technorati take their seats for Facebook founder, Mark Zuckerberg, to take the stage for his scheduled 10 a.m. keynote address during Facebook's third annual developer conference.

At 10:11 a.m., Zuckerberg walks onstage, wearing his signature black, zip-up hoodie sweatshirt, dark wash jeans, and a pop-star microphone adhered to the side of his face.[137]

During this opening keynote, Zuckerberg will introduce defining characteristics of the Facebook platform that will not only change our vocabulary for talking about internet generated content, but also change what we—as audiences—expect from internet content: "instantly social experiences in every website, every application and everywhere you go," like social media plugins that allow us to like, share, and recommend content on websites outside of Facebook.com—without ever needing to sign in to the platform.[138]

"We are building a Web where the default is social," Zuckerberg says.[139] And boy did they ever.

It all started in the 1600s, with the origins of print media.

From the first newspaper publication, print media has served as "objective" record, chronicling the day's news. In

137 Schoenfeld, "Zuckerberg: 'Web Where the Default is Social,'" April 21, 2010.
138 Ibid.
139 Ibid.

the United States in particular, print media evolved over the years from its revolutionary founding principles and assigned itself the responsibility of objective arbiter of current events. For centuries, print media—affectionately referred to as the fourth estate—sought to provide unbiased access to information that had the power to unite the public in times of triumph and despair.

Over time, the role of media evolved and adapted to public demand.

Today, much of our media content promotes our consumer interests. It shapes and perpetuates global trends. You see, we wouldn't remark that a certain style was "en vogue" if the design did not actually appear in *Vogue*.

Media has adapted to the pace of information sharing. With the rise of broadcast media, followed by the dawn of the internet, media has had to adapt from an editorial tradition with a determination to curate "all the news that's fit to print" to a high-speed race to commentary, rooted in the initiative to report quickly and fact check later.

Over the past decade, we've seen major media brands ingrained in the ethos of our country shutter and board up their doors. Facing slumping ad sales, reductions in circulation, and a dramatic expansion in online publishing, print outlets have needed to consider new revenue streams and partnership with brands to keep their outlets afloat. Consider one of the most storied publishers in American history—TIME Inc.

ABOUT TIME

Founded in 1922 by Henry Luce and Briton Hadden, Time Inc. became one of America's first mass media corporations, carrying worldwide influence. The company merged with Warner Communications in 1990 to form Time Warner.

At the height of its success, the corporation had grown to publish more than one hundred magazine brands—ranging from its namesake *Time* magazine, to the iconic pictorial magazine *Life*, to business magazines like *Fortune*, and extending to human interest publications including *People*, *Entertainment Weekly*, and *Sports Illustrated*.

But print media has always been cyclical and TIME Inc. regularly weathered trials. Its first major disruption came in the 1950s with the introduction of broadcast television, but nothing could have prepared the company for the dot-com boom of the 1990s. The internet enabled an explosion of choice in media consumption.

Readership hit an all-time high, with users consuming news across many devices at home, at work, and on the go. But this democratized access to publishing platforms cut into the authority and value of print media as arbiter of the national record. And, the biggest blow to traditional media—a blow from which it is unclear it will ever fully recover—comes in the form of advertising revenue.

In the words of storied media mogul Rupert Murdoch, advertising revenue once represented "rivers of gold" flowing profits across his newspapers.[140] The challenge is as simple as the principles of supply and demand. The total, available, purchasable space ballooned overnight, but the total number of advertisers remained constant.

So, fast forward through Y2K and now we've got a problem. In 2003, when Google introduced "Adsense," effectively turning anyone with an internet connection into a "publisher" able to sell advertising space, in ways that would be more "targeted" or "personalized" or "niche" than would a pre-printed ad in, let's say, *Time* Magazine. This simple switch in mentality caused the value of ads to plummet, effectively eliminating that river of gold that had fueled the growth and dominance of print media for decades. Their river of gold had dried up. [141]

In addition to volume and access, these new mediums created challenges that traditional media simply couldn't counter. Television and the internet both bring news to the consumer faster and in a more visually engaging way than newspapers will ever be able to. Print is entirely constrained by their physical format, their print processes, and once-daily (or once-weekly, or even *GASP* monthly, for magazines) distribution.

Which brings us to 2004. The Boston Red Sox win their first World Series since 1918 and Ciara introduced us to the term "goodies." These are the highlights, really. But something else

---

140 Edgecliffe-Johnson, "Murdoch predicts the demise of classified ads," November 24, 2005.

141 Pew Research Center. "Newspapers Fact Sheet." July 9, 2019.

happened in 2004 that would dramatically change the future of media—Mark Zuckerberg introduced TheFacebook.

THE ORIGINS OF THEFACEBOOK

Visualize it: Big hair. Lace. Spandex and leg warmers. Shoulder pads and so much neon. What's that you hear? The sounds of Freddie Mercury, David Bowie, Madonna, and Blondie. Yup, we're in the '80s. [Of note, I never experienced the '80s. Being born in 1990 is actually one of the greatest disappointments of my life, because I think would have loved the '80s, based almost exclusively on my love for the VH1 show *I Love the '80s* and enjoyment of bars where '80s cover bands play.]

It was during this incredible decade the internet really took off. It started with fairly low functionality message boards. Bulletin board systems, BBS, for short, enabled file sharing, group chatting, and direct messaging between users. These systems are were largely distributors for pirated software and games. The "primitive" nature of technology during the '80s limited the functionality of these systems, but they opened the worldwide web's eyes to the possibilities of the internet.

Further, they gave way to widespread access to a technology called email, which gave way to the dawn of America Online (AOL), the true precursor to the social networking sites we've come to know and love, at the close of the 1980s. And just like that, AOL became synonymous with the '90s.

AOL was service like we had never seen before. It was an umbrella platform that introduced subscription-based internet, access to multiplayer gaming, a bespoke internet search engine, dedicated content channels, and provided the basis for *You've Got Mail*, the greatest romantic comedy ever filmed.

And by the mid-1990s, the internet's engines were firing on all cylinders. Opportunity seemed endless. In January 2000, AOL and—you'll never guess—Time Warner announced plans to merge. The deal closed on January 11, 2001. By 2003, AOL Time Warner dropped the "AOL" from its name.

And back on the 'net, a variety of new social networking sites were budding.

Classmates.com became a hit by offering to help users reconnect with former schoolmates via virtual reunion. Classmates.com was followed by SixDegrees.com, which encouraged users to create profiles and invite friends to join the platform, organize groups, and network with other users. But social media really hit its stride with the launch of Friendster, which promoted "real" online communities where users declared their "circles of friends" for others on the platform.

I first learned of Friendster, and a handful of other sites gaining popularity around the same time— Myspace and Facebook—during an episode of *The Daily Show With Jon Stewart* in 2006.

Comedian Demetri Martin, Senior Youth Correspondent for *The Daily Show*, regularly performed a segment called "Trendspotting."[142] During this segment, he broke down the

---

142 Martin, *The Daily Show With Jon Stewart*. "Trendspotting: Social Networking." February 15, 2006.

basics of social networking sites, a trend that had exploded onto the scene and continued to gain popularity among younger internet users.

"The hottest new trend is social networking online. This youth phenomenon is getting hotter by the minute," Martin states. And then he pauses. "Even in that pause right there, it even got a little hotter."[143]

"So, what are social networking sites," he continues. "Well first of all, if you don't know, you're a loser."[144]

The segment goes on to highlight Facebook, "which is for students," Martin states as he types in "kind of a student" in the user field of the Facebook homepage, Myspace, which then had more than 50,000,000 users, and Friendster, which fizzled out early in the social media boom.[145]

Myspace was once the "darling" of the social media world. It started as a domain for bands to advertise their music, but as Martin observes in his segment on *The Daily Show*, it soon became a way for youths "to advertise themselves."[146] These sites enabled users to build their own self-portraits by plugging in basic information and customizing a profile template. Through a username, 'about me' section, and in-profile music, and imagery selections, users determined exactly what others who navigate to their page would understand about them as people.

---

143 Ibid.
144 Ibid.
145 Ibid.
146 Ibid.

These tools for self-made celebrity, however, were not entirely focused on the users' content. In fact, the main draw—at least for users, like me, in their teens—was the ability to promote your entourage through the 'Top 8' friends functionality.

Remember how I mentioned building celebrity was all about networking?

Myspace made your close network a matter of public interest. In the templatized profile that Myspace provided its users, profile builders had the ability to advertise their eight best friends for all to see, and further let other users know exactly where you stood in the social pecking order.

Even further, it gave other users the ability to determine *just how close* you really were to your Top 8 friends.

If you listed Sara as your best friend, you better pray to Britney Spears that Sara keeps you in her #1 spot too. Being taken out of a friend's Top 8 was the ultimate insult and, arguably, the precursor to *Mean Girl's* Gretchen Wieners', "YOU CAN'T SIT WITH US!"[147] This time, though, it would be a public social media shaming.

But even the popularity of Myspace, which warranted faux news segments on Comedy Central, couldn't have prepared us for the Facebook takeover that would follow.

Facebook started as a site exclusively open to Harvard University students. It was soon opened to a select set of elite schools

---

147 Waters, dir. *Mean Girls*. 2004.

deemed worthy of participating, making it all the more popular and desirable to be on. And then, in 2006, Facebook opened to the general public. By 2009, Silicon Valley venture capitalist (and founder of PayPal), Peter Thiel invested millions of dollars in the project and sat back to watch it grow. As of March 2020, Facebook boasts more than 2.6 billion monthly active users. [148]

What really allowed for Facebook to take off was the introduction of an open API in 2007, known as the Facebook Platform, which made it possible for third-party software and application developers to create new apps that would operate within Facebook itself. Essentially, by opening up the platform to developers, Facebook turned itself into the mall of the internet. The destination where all of the cool kids could go to mingle.

Within early days of the API release, the platform gained a massive amount of attention. Hundreds of thousands of apps were developed on the Facebook platform. It was so popular that Facebook even launched the Facebook App Store to help users browse them all.

Seeing the success of Facebook, Twitter, which launched in 2006 around the time that a fifteen-year-old Clare Carluccio was learning about Myspace on Comedy Central, released its own API and saw similar success follow. And that was all it took.

By 2009, social media had overtaken pornography as the #1 use of the internet,[149] validating the sage Demetri Martin's

---

148 Statista. "Number of monthly active Facebook users worldwide as of 1st quarter 2020 (in millions)." April 30, 2020.

149 Goldsmith. "Study: Social Networking Sites Overtake Porn As Internet's #1 Search." *Reuters*. October 18, 2008.

comedic prediction that "online networking" had surpassed "promiscuous sex" on a chart of "things that young people like the most."[150] And by 2010, when Facebook introduced the social plugins that would enable us to like, share, and recommend any content from around the internet on our own personal Facebook pages, social media companies truly saw what the platforms were capable of: hyper-targeted advertisements that would cause social media networks to grow at light speed.

Given the early phenomena that was social media, we should have read the writing on the wall for traditional media brands. But there was one factor missing in 2006 that prohibited our ability to predict how all-encompassing social media would become. We didn't have smart phones.

THE MOBILITY OF SOCIAL NETWORKS

Mobile computing arrived in the mid-90s with the introduction of the Palm Pilot, a handheld PC marketed to the office workers of the world. But the concept really took off in 2007 with the introduction of the Apple iPhone. This high-tech device was designed for the everyday user. Its touchscreen interface was easy to navigate. It put the power of the internet in the palm of our hand. It built on lessons learned from the successes of AOL and social media and delivered a complete app store allowing users to browse, select, and download new apps to customize their mobile experiences.

---

150 Martin, *The Daily Show With Jon Stewart*. "Trendspotting: Social Networking." February 15, 2006.

What's more? The iPhone made simple photo and video-sharing applications. These were critical to the success of social networking sites, and even provided the basis for the launch of new social media applications, including Instagram and Snapchat (two platforms that leveraged the captive Facebook audience to build their own user bases).

Photo and video sharing platforms have collected more than 20 billion images since the introduction of Instagram, and the images have been generated almost exclusively on mobile devices.[151]

They have also inspired mobile social media users to get more creative about the ways in which they engage their audiences. They delivered new tools to a planet of creators.

The varied user behaviors of these platforms and their reach enable users to tailor their content on each platform and knit the personalities together to build an overarching, digital identity—one that doesn't need to track directly to the user's personal identity.

What had happened in this span is that the rise of third-party apps, social media giants, and the dynamic shifts in the way that users consumed content sent traditional media into a tailspin.

Then, the 2008 financial crisis hit, and traditional media companies took yet another damaging blow as advertising budgets all but vanished, the losses taking jobs with them on

---

151 Gold. "Who Killed Time Inc.," February 1, 2018.

their way out the door. By 2010, Time Inc.'s operating income fell to $515 million, half of what it was five years earlier.[152]

And, back on the 'net, the popularity of the world wide web had exploded, and Time Warner found itself completed disrupted. Activist investor, Carl Icahn, purchased $2 billion in Time Warner stock and demanded the company begin restructuring to right the ship.[153]

Time Inc. spun out AOL in 2009, the first company under the conglomerate they let go.[154] Then, they spun out Time Warner Cable in 2012.[155] As stated by a reporter to the Columbia Journalism Review, following these divestitures, "Time Inc. now had a target on its back."[156]

Terry McDonell, who led Time Inc.'s sports group wrote in his memoir that he believed that the Time Warner leadership always planned to "dump Time Inc." so that the company could focus on growing Turner, Warner Bros., HBO, and cable: "Where the real money was."[157] But, while he still had oversight of the media conglomerate, Jeff Bewkes pushed Time Inc. to digitize.

By 2012, video was king. The industry saw a number of acquisitions of video platforms by the reigning social media

---

152 Ibid.
153 Stone and Flahretty, "Icahn buying up Time Warner shares: sources," January 11, 2016.
154 Gold. "Who Killed Time Inc.," February 1, 2018.
155 Ibid.
156 Ibid.
157 Ibid.

platforms—in attempt to protect their relevance—and video-fueled media companies, including BuzzFeed and Mashable, started to drive viral online content and steal shares of voice from major media brands.

CEO Jeff Bewkes noted that the split would allow Time Warner to focus entirely on its television and film businesses, and Time Inc. to focus on its core print media businesses.[158] They announced in May 2014 that Time Inc. would become a publicly traded company on June 6 of that year, and the spin-off was completed on June 9, 2014.

It appeared to almost everyone inside and observing the media industry that, at least for the moment, new media had won. But in reality, in the social media space where business was seemingly booming, it wasn't all sunshine and rainbows.

For Facebook and Twitter, it was quite the opposite, actually.

By 2015, Twitter's growth had stagnated, and Facebook saw a decline in user engagement. User feeds had become dominated by viral videos, memes, GIFs, and clickbait, which made it harder for users to genuinely engage. It made voyeurs out of most users.[159]

That same year, however, Time Inc. took another hit. It abandoned the storied Time-Life building in midtown Manhattan for a lower-rent, up-and-coming space in the

---

158 Ibid.
159 Comscore. "2016 U.S. Cross-Platform Future in Focus" March 30, 2016.

financial district of New York City. And, lest you think this move would signal defeat for the storied brand, it did not.

In fact, Time Inc. saw the growing pains being reported extensively around social media as an opportunity to reclaim some mind share with audiences; companies began launching video and social platforms left and right.

In 2016, Time Inc., under the new executive direction of Rich Battista, introduced a holistic turnaround program, which spanned cost reductions and introduction of new revenue streams. The latter was a priority of Time Inc.'s external narrative.

Battista regularly stated that the team at Time Inc. was taking a portion of its cost savings and reinvesting it for growth, specifically in new platforms and in areas of branded content and advertising, video, television, and live events. The company introduced Time Inc. Productions and attempted to launch a handful of television shows. Further, the media company announced that it would acquire Viant, a leading marketing platform and owner of Myspace.

These efforts appeared—at least initially—to be helping.

In Battista's first year at the helm of Time Inc., he established the company within the top ten digital audiences of online media properties, according to ComScore's monthly U.S. multi-platform report for December 2016, sharing leadership with Google and Facebook, a metric that would have been seemingly unheard of one year prior.[160]

Time Inc.'s investment in digital and mobile content enabled the platform to reach 128.8 million unique monthly visitors, a 13 percent increase in audience year-over-year, which included a 23 percent year-over-year increase in the number of users who visited Time Inc. via mobile devices.

By the end of 2016, nearly 80 percent of Time Inc.'s consumers came from mobile devices, a major shakeup for the storied print media company. But, despite this aggressive campaign and a fair amount of investment (successful investment, might I add), Time Inc. continued to falter.

And, in November 2017, it was announced that the Meredith Corporation would acquire Time Inc. and its subsidiaries. The deal closed in January of 2018, and former editorial director of Time Inc. John Huey tweeted— because, of course he did—"R.I.P. Time Inc. The 95-year run is over."[161]

In the years since the sale of Time Inc. to Meredith Corporation, the company has continued to publish its array of magazines and online news, but the struggle continues. And Time is just one of many storied brands undergoing similar challenges. Every month, headlines herald mass layoffs or restructuring from publications ranging from

---

160 Ibid.
161 Huey. Twitter Post. January 31, 2018.

regional newspapers to brands under the umbrella of Condé Nast, largely driven by shifting attentions, social platforms, and overwhelming access to content.

Since the start of the COVID-19 pandemic, a number of reporters I work with regularly have been laid off from their positions, and some of the stories I was supporting were cut from the print issue as major publications lost more than forty-five pages in advertising revenue.

But I highly doubt we'll see Mark Zuckerberg shedding tears for the media industry any soon, because social media sites, and the users who create content for them, have provided a booming new outlet for advertisers.

WHERE SHOULD WE PLACE OUR TRUST?

In a post-social media world, I think we need to adapt the shortcuts we have traditionally invoked to help us determine what information we deem trustworthy and what we will allow to influence our own decision making.

The challenge is that these psychological factors have been established over mere decades of human interaction. But, when we established these cultural norms and guidelines for credibility, we didn't foresee that many social media users would be willing to create content for broader consumption.

What's more, we couldn't have anticipated how effectively this user-generated content would blur the line between the real and the fake.

"Influencers are just modern-day marketing products," says Chavie Lieber, a reporter for The Business of Fashion, focused on the influencer industry.[162] The question for marketers is, as Lieber argues, "Who can push product the best? It's like these characters who live on the internet and have incredible following are able to push product better than any form of marketing we've previously seen."[163]

And, what we're seeing more and more every day is the expansion beyond simple product marketing in disguise, with influencers dipping their toes into the waters of advocacy and activism.

And as this content becomes more pervasive, it becomes harder for us—as consumers—to remember that it is editorial, not necessarily fact-checked, reporting.

---

162 Sanders, "The New Celebrity," September 10, 2019.
163 Ibid.

7

PERFORMING REALITY

I initially started working on this book because I found myself referring to my plans for weeknight evenings as "heading home to catch up with my friends from *Southern Charm*, Cameron and Shep." Or—if I missed an episode of *The Real Housewives of New York*, saying: "It's been so long since I've heard from Sonja." Now, I think we can all agree that I watch too much reality television, but most of these comments were made in jest, and my overindulgence in reality television does not take away from its importance as a case study for influence. If anything, I think it adds to it.

As stated in her aptly titled book, *Reality TV*, June Deery reflects that to dismiss the importance of reality television on our culture and society is to completely miss its significance. She writes, "reality TV is important in the most basic terms because it pervades TV schedules around the world and has, as a consequence, entered all kinds of popular and elite discourse, from personal blogs to presidential politics."[164]

---

164 Deery, *Reality TV*, Page 1.

How many times have you heard the criticism that we've undermined the power of the American Presidency by electing a reality star to the White House?

Well, it's true. Donald Trump is the most powerful democratic, talentless celebrity that we have ever encountered.

Donald Trump was born in Queens to a family of real estate moguls. His rise to the national scene was driven by early successes in business, and then branded when he launched his book, *The Art of the Deal*, in 1987. But his continued relevance from Hollywood to Washington DC was largely driven by the same tactics of the democratic star I've been exploring throughout this book.

It started with networking. In fact, in a map of the most elite celebrity social network—that of *Vogue* Magazine's Editor in Chief, Anna Wintour—Elizabeth Currid-Halket of USC identified Donald Trump right in the middle of the pack. And, what's more, Currid-Halkett identified Trump as a "boundary spanner" in Wintour's network, meaning he was strongly connected to not only the A-listers in Wintour's world, but also to leaders from industry and politics.[165] Essentially, anywhere there was potential to influence, Donald Trump was present.

But, beyond his network, Donald Trump's celebrity is characterized by its excess. His celebrity residual draws reference from his relationships over the years with gorgeous women, his association with the Miss Universe

---

165 USC Price, "Starstruck Literary Luncheon," May 12, 2011.

pageant, and—most notably—his reality TV persona on *The Apprentice.*

He used every form of media available to him during a pre-social media time to curate a luxurious image that promoted him as a highly successful man in business, raking in the spoils that come with market excellence.

But Donald Trump's celebrity permanence was solidified with his entrance to Twitter.

In an op-ed for *The New York Times*, TV critic James Poniewozik wrote of Trump that "when he adopted social media, he used it like TV. First, he used it like a celebrity, to broadcast himself, his first tweet in 2009 promoting a *Late Show with David Letterman* appearance. Then he used it like an instigator, tweeting his birther conspiracies before he would talk about them on Fox News, road-testing his call for a border wall during the cable-news fueled Ebola and border panics of the 2014 midterms."[166]

But it was when he became a Presidential candidate, Poniewozik continues, that Trump mastered the art of Twitter for the broadest possible reach. He says: "His tweets programmed TV and were amplified by it. On *CNBC*, a 'BREAKING NEWS: TRUMP TWEET' graphic would spin out onscreen as soon as the words left his thumbs. He would watch Fox News, or Lou Dobbs, or CNN, or *Morning*

166 Poniewozik, "OPINION: Real Donald Trump is Character on TV," *September 6, 2019.*

Joe, or *Saturday Night Live,* and get mad, and tweet. Then the tweets would become TV, and he would watch it, and tweet again."[167]

He managed to turn his actual life into reality television programming.

As a category, reality TV is described as unscripted drama, non-fictional programming, and factual entertainment. "Factual entertainment strikes me as appropriate," states Deery, "when factual indicates something actually occurring at a particular place and time, not necessarily objectively represented or scientifically verifiable."[168]

It's obvious—I hope—to those of us watching reality television that the programs adopt some of the conventions of traditional theater and scripted television. The producers and editors shape the audiences' experience of the reality we observe, both by orchestrating volatile situations that they film as they unfold and in post-production, enhancing scenes with emotive music, cutting dialogue to create dramatic irony and leaving viewers with cliff hangers that will ensure we tune in the following week.

For this reason, Deery describes Reality TV as "staged actuality," acknowledging more directly the performance aspects required for it to actually exist.[169]

---

167 Ibid.
168 Deery, *Reality TV*, Page 49.
169 Deery, *Reality TV*, Page 29.

MIRRORING REALITY

Since the origins of theater, performance has existed for the benefit of the audience. It is intended to entertain, to inform, and to comment on the off-stage world. You see, most performance is intended to be a reflection of a culture at a particular moment in time, and it is up to the performers (and their directors, producers, and editors) to bring that moment to life for audiences.

This first clicked for me years ago when I was lucky enough to see a performance of William Shakespeare's *Merchant of Venice* directed by Rupert Goold and performed by players from the Royal Shakespeare Company.[170]

The Merchant is largely known as William Shakespeare's "problem play." It is formatted as a comedy but has some incredibly disturbing plot lines and comes together at the very end in a bit of a haphazard manner, rare for a Shakespearean narrative.

The story focuses on a merchant named Antonio and his friend Bassiano, who is desperately in love with an heiress named Portia. But, Portia is fated to marry whichever man travels out to her estate and participates in a guessing game of chance that her father created to protect Portia's fortune before he passed. In order to court Portia, Bassiano needs money and he asks Antonio for a loan. However, Antonio's money is caught up in a number of shipping ventures, so he seeks a loan from a Jewish moneylender called Shylock.

---

170 Shakespeare, *The Merchant of Venice*, dir. Rupert Goold, Performed by The Royal Shakespeare Company, Stratford Upon Avon, U.K., July 2011.

Antonio acts as Bassiano's guarantor for the loan, but—for reasons not actually explained in the play—Shylock really does not like Antonio. The only collateral Shylock will accept in turn for the loan plus interest is a pound of Antonio's flesh.[171]

It's a ridiculous premise. It has the makings of a modern soap opera—unrequited love, passion, discrimination, loans sharks—so obviously it's one of my favorites.

Shakespeare brought this story to life in the Italian port city because at the time it was known as a fairly shady place. Venice was characterized by transient merchants, known for loose morality; while few actually lived there, many passed through. Essentially, it was somewhere that the audience of Elizabethan England could have imagined this ridiculous premise might actually take place. But today, we think of Venice as that romantic city in Northern Italy with singing gondoliers and beautiful, sinking architecture. So, plop the narrative of *The Merchant of Venice* in Las Vegas, just as Goold did in 2011, and you have a perfect historical parallel.[172]

Where else are loan sharks casually acknowledged around town? Las Vegas brings to life the mix of romantic fantasy meets showbiz meets capitalism that only reads true to a modern audience in a city known to conceal all that happens there.

---

171 Shakespeare, *The Merchant of Venice,* 1600.
172 Shakespeare, *The Merchant of Venice*, dir. Rupert Goold, July 2011.

So, it is with the context of "what happens in Vegas, stays in Vegas," that a modern audience can truly understand the seediness of the dealings between Antonio and Shylock. In addition to plopping *The Merchant* into the middle of the Nevada desert, Goold recast the crazy game of chance that defined Portia's romantic fate into something much more reasonable to a modern audience: a reality TV competition.[173]

Just as we see ourselves in the democratic celebrities we watch on Bravo, we are urged to identify ourselves in the characters of any stage performance.

This concept inspired an entire field of academia: Performance Studies.

The principle's founder, Richard Schechner, defined the discipline in two categories: Artistic and Cultural Performance. Artistic performances are designated as art forms, including performance art, poetry, theatrical plays, concerts, dramatic readings, and so on. Cultural performance, on the other hand, refers to events that occur daily and demonstrate the values of a culture—parades, religious ceremonies, festivals, news reporting/storytelling, as well as individual performances of race, gender, sexuality, class, social structure, and profession.[174]

The cultural resonance of performance can be most tangibly felt when watching a revival of a show that first premiered during another generation.

---

173   Ibid.
174   Schechner, *Performance Theory*, 1977.

Take, for example, Bartlett Sher's rendition of *My Fair Lady* at Lincoln Center in 2018. Over the years, we have grown to know Eliza Doolittle and Henry Higgins like old friends. We anticipate the class issues that initially separate the two lead characters, we anticipate the personal chemistry that will magnetically draw the two together, and we are heartbroken at the stubbornness and bullying attitude that comes to separate them again. But, in earlier performances of the show, we see that Eliza, despite being able to "stand on [her] own," comes back to Henry, and we as an audience largely accepted that the two were fated to be together.[175]

But, drop this plot into a modern culture shining a bright spotlight on gender equality and harassment, and Henry's bullying becomes a lot harder for an audience to forgive. In fact, it would actually feel foolish to hope Eliza would go back to Henry after their last argument. This is, perhaps, the reason that Sher's revival took the story back to its original conclusion, where Eliza truly does leave Henry to stand on her own.[176]

Eliza transforms, in that moment, from the character who learned the manners of society so she could marry well and blend into the crowd into a resourceful woman who worked her way out of an unfavorable situation, learned the skills she would need to start over, and made the decision to go out on her own the moment she recognized she hit a ceiling in her progress. Rather than the archetypal female lead in a marriage plot, she becomes the embodiment of self-sufficiency.

---

175 Lerner, *My Fair Lady,* dir. Bartlett Sher, Lincoln Center Theater, March 2018–July 2019.
176 Ibid.

But, this social commentary only lands because we are expecting a certain outcome from the archetype itself.

It wasn't until I started working on this book that I realized how far performance theory can extend beyond the theater.

Reality television—be it *The Apprentice* or *Keeping Up With the Kardashians*—adopts many of the conventions we've come to understand through theater and fiction, specifically leveraging archetypal characters, recurrent examples of personality "types" that regularly pop up in all kinds of content.

Subconsciously, we associate the characters the producers of reality programs have created through the editing process with archetypes we've previously seen, and we come to expect the same outcome from these characters as a result.

On *The Bachelor*, we know that the girl who comes off as spoiled in the promo will most likely become that season's villain and, on the other end of the spectrum, we instinctively root for the small town girl who has never been kissed because she seems like the wholesome Disney princess the show's format promises will win.

Celebrity-driven reality TV operates in the same fashion. *Keeping Up With the Kardashians* utilizes the archetypes of a family sitcom to structure life in the Kardashian-Jenner household. Kris is the matriarch and lead decision maker; she is 2019's Carol Brady. Kim is the favorite, the sister who seems to walk in the sun no matter where she goes. Yup, you guessed it, Kim is Marcia. That makes Khloe the down-on-her-luck middle child who can never seem to catch a break. Welcome to the family, Jan.

See? And now even if you're a Baby Boomer and have never watched an episode of the Kardashians, you know what to expect from an episode. Alternatively? If you're a millennial and never had the opportunity to watch Nick@Nite, you are now culturally informed. You're welcome.

STAGING HISTORY

Iconic. That' is the only word to describe Jackie Kennedy. After marrying into the Kennedy family in 1953, Jackie became a staple at Jack Kennedy's side—in politics and in society. When the Kennedys moved into the White House, Jackie became third-youngest First Lady in history, and she was certainly the first to transform the role of first lady to the highly visible platform it is today.

Early on in the Kennedys political career, Jackie saw the power of her role and ability to shape the narrative that followed her and her husband. In addition to being absolutely beautiful in an age where television was beginning to define mass media, Jackie Kennedy was a socialite and her status transformed the role of the First Lady from the woman supporting the President to celebrity status.

Jackie quickly became a trendsetter. Her brightly colored outfits, pillbox hats, and well-tailored suits made her look as if she had just stepped out of a fashion magazine; women across the country lined up at department stores to purchase her perfect look.

But Jackie's role as fashion influencer is only one piece of the puzzle.

In addition, Jackie was the first of the First Ladies to hire a press secretary and carefully cultivate her relationship with the reporters on the White House press corps. Her attention to the Kennedy image allowed her to artfully edit the story being told externally. It has been said that Jackie would personally edit reporters' articles following interviews she participated in before they went to print. She hand-selected the imagery that the public would see of the family as they traveled, and through this high-touch curation, she built her image as the icon we know conjure in our collective memory.[177]

Just one week following John F. Kennedy's assassination, Jackie gave an interview to *Life* magazine, during which she shaped her husband's presidential legacy for posterity.

SPINNING CAMELOT
When Jackie Kennedy invited Theodore H. White to her home in Hyannis Port, Massachusetts, she took the first step toward cementing her husband's legacy. In a memoir written about the interview, White describes the experience interviewing the newly widowed First Lady, describing her

---

177 Ostergaard, "Jackie Kennedy Onassis: An Icon for the Ages." CommonLit. 2018.

as "obsessed" with the notion that her husband be remembered as a hero.[178]

"Quite inadvertently, I was her instrument in labeling the myth," White confesses.[179]

White, you see, was one of the "friendly" reporters that Jackie had cultivated a relationship with during her time in the White House and, over the years, she had given White access to the Kennedy family, in turn further engendering his kind coverage. It was Jackie Kennedy's wish that White publish the essay resulting from their interview in *Life* magazine, because that was also the publication that chronicled the couple's wedding, her husband's Presidential Inauguration, and profiles of the Kennedy children. But, most importantly, *Life* had been known to publish the stories and images that defined history.

Throughout the interview, Jackie bounced back and forth from gruesome accounts of the assassination to musings on the Kennedys' time in the White House and responses to rumors of what she would do now that her husband had died. The sporadic conversation flow is captured in White's resulting essay, as well as in his handwritten notes later dedicated to the Kennedy archives.

But, throughout it all, Jackie made clear the theatrical archetype she wanted her husband to been associated with for decades to come. He was the tragic hero.

---

178 Sydney, "Camelot." *The Kennedy Assassination Chronicles*, Fall 1995.

179 Ibid.

In the resulting piece, Jackie talks about history and the role that history played in creating Jack's idealism.

"You must think of him as this little boy, sick so much of the time, reading in bed, reading history, reading the Knights of the Round Table...For Jack, history was full of heroes. And if it made him this way—if it made him see the heroes—maybe other little boys will see...Jack had this hero idea of history, the idealistic view."[180]

And so, Jackie outlines her own version of history for posterity—a version separate from those that would be written in "dusty or bitter histories," as she described them, which she was sure would soon follow.[181]

"When Jack quoted something, it was usually classical," she said, "but I'm so ashamed of myself—all I keep thinking of is this line from a musical comedy. At night, before we'd go to sleep, Jack liked to play some records; and the song he loved most came at the very end of this record. The lines he loved to hear were: don't let it be forgot, that once there was a spot, for one brief shining moment that was known as Camelot."[182]

A point she reiterated multiple times throughout the interview. "There'll be great Presidents again—and the Johnsons are wonderful, they've been wonderful to me—but there'll never be another Camelot again."[183]

---

180 White, "For President Kennedy: An Epilogue," December 6, 1963.
181 Sydney, "Camelot" *The Kennedy Assassination Chronicles,* Fall 1995.
182 White, "For President Kennedy: An Epilogue," December 6, 1963.
183 Ibid.

In this framing, Jackie likens the Kennedy presidency to a heroic tale of the Knights of the Round table, a new brotherhood of knights who wouldn't pillage and fight, but rather work to uphold honor, justice, and idealism.

And when she finishes speaking, she sends White into the study, and gives him forty-five minutes to transcribe the interview and edit his essay.

"She certainly wanted to take control of history," said presidential historian Stephen E. Ambrose, a critic of the rose-colored portrayals of the Kennedy years, "and in so many ways she managed to do so."[184]

Much of the substance of the Camelot interview appeared in the *Life* essay, "For President Kennedy: An Epilogue." The magazine held the presses that November night, at a cost of $30,000 an hour for overtime, while Mr. White talked with Mrs. Kennedy. He finally dictated his story to editors from the telephone in the Kennedy kitchen at 2 a.m., with Jackie Kennedy standing nearby, listening in.[185]

And when his editors suggested that White had over-played the Camelot theme in the resulting piece, Jackie—listening to the dictation—shook her head and made him fight to keep it in. In White's words, Jackie wanted him to "rescue Jack from all these 'bitter people' who were going to write about him in history. She did not want Jack left to the historians."[186]

---

184 Baer, "JFK The Mystique of Camelot," May 27, 1995.
185 Sydney, "Camelot," The Kennedy Assassination Chronicles Fall 1995.
186 Ibid.

"It is astounding to me that a week after JFK's death, she had the presence of mind to come up with the extraordinary and unexpected reference that has stuck with us for decades," says screenwriter Noah Oppenheim, who wrote the movie *Jackie*, which is based on this exact interview.[187]

It certainly is astounding. I cannot imagine the emotional trauma that Jackie Kennedy experienced that week. But you can't help but wonder, there may never be Camelot again, but was there ever really Camelot for the Kennedys?

More objective views of history tell us stories of a fairly broken family, complete with unhappy marriages that were characterized by infidelity, suspicion, resentment, tragic deaths, and drug abuse. But in a moment of national trauma, who are we—the audience—to question Jackie Kennedy's own account of their life.

Through her Camelot interview, Jackie Kennedy solidified her own staged actuality for the history books.

REAL, RAW, AND HIGHLY PRODUCED

Today, our popular acceptance of "staged actuality" spotlights a paradox our own cultural fabric: the tendency of Americans to push for "real" and "unfiltered" content, while fully allowing ourselves to suspend disbelief for entertaining leisure content.

---

187 McAfee and McNeil, "How Jackie Kennedy Invented Camelot," November 22, 2017.

We want to watch the "real," but only in so far as it feels nostalgic and authentic to what we have come to expect from the stories we are told. Which brings us back to the importance of the performative. The unscripted nature of reality makes it more challenging to control the narrative, but onscreen staged elements can influence how the audience reads a situation.

And the impact of this perception extends well beyond our understanding of characters on a show. When it comes to reality TV, we build personas around the characters. We tune in beyond the program itself to track the latest happenings in tabloids, keep tabs on their day-to-day across social media, and build out impressions of their character in our minds.

To take us back to June Deery's observations on reality TV, "Online extensions of TV broadcasts are becoming an increasingly vital component for all involved—producers, viewers and participants—and the ontological, psychological, and commercial repercussions of this expansion require more analysis."[188]

So, in the case of Donald Trump, we have an inclination to associate his persona with the decisive businessman we once watched on *The Apprentice.* The facts of his career, his track record, didn't really matter all that much in forming his political perception (at least during the election). Many Americans were able to accept the shortcut of their experience with his character and allow that background to tag him as archetypal highly successful manager.

---

188 Deery, *Reality TV,* Page 73.

With the dramatic expansion of reality television—and the way that similar qualities of democratic celebrity have seeped well beyond the filters of traditional media and onto the internet—we are faced with a responsibility we haven't previously encountered. We, the audience, need to assess the authority of the characters we're observing.

8

OUR LOOSE CONNECTIONS

Now, you may put this book down between chapters and think to yourself—okay, so what? There are thousands of people in the world willing to shamelessly push product over their Instagram feeds and rake in the cash. Kylie Jenner did it so well she became a ~~billionaire~~ $900 million-aire.

What's new here? The advertising industry has always pushed product to consumers.

But the reason I am so fascinated by this trend is that the way these products, people, ideas, and trends are being delivered is highly personal in an era where in-person interpersonal communication is at an extreme low.

Looking back again to America in the 1800s, community engagement was a major aspect of daily life. De Tocqueville observed that structures like mass-media (newspapers, really) would likely serve as tools to support community life.

In fact, he wrote that newspapers were perhaps Americans' only hope for sustaining civic engagement in a world advancing toward individualism.

He wrote: "When no firm and lasting ties any longer unite men, it is impossible to obtain the cooperation of any great number of them unless you can persuade every man whose help is required that he serves his private interests by voluntarily uniting his efforts to those of all the others. That cannot be done habitually and conveniently without the help of a newspaper. Only a newspaper can put the same thought as the same time before a thousand readers...So hardly any democratic association can carry on without a newspaper."[189]

And, in some senses he was right. Mass media does have the unique capability of distributing content, to put the same perspective in front of many eyes at the same time.

But what happens when there are millions of newspapers?

As media expands, from newspapers to television to the internet and all of its niche pockets, mass media content has created an environment in which each consumer can—in a sense—chose their own adventure and only consume the content they find most engaging.

SPLINTERING ATTENTION

At the start of the new millennium, sociologist Robert Putnam published a book titled *Bowling Alone: The Collapse and*

---

189 Putnam, *Bowling Alone*, Page 218.

Revival of American Community. In his research, Putnam argued that—just as de Tocqueville predicted—American communities were waning. Individualism and isolationism were on the rise and, in many ways, the proliferation of entertainment content and mass media was driving the trend forward.

Putnam wrote, "When the history of the twentieth century is written with greater perspective than we now enjoy, the impact of technology on communications and leisure will almost surely be a major theme. At the beginning of the century the communications and entertainment industries hardly existed outside small publishing houses and music halls. The first quarter of the century had nearly passed before the term mass media was invented. At the end of the century by contrast, the gradual merger of the massive telecommunications and entertainment industries had become the very foundation for a new economic era."[190]

He looked at two major trends in content driving American civic disengagement:[191]

1. **The rise of personalized news and entertainment platforms**—Putnam recognized that the expansion of television content means that communities no longer need to align on tastes and interests in order to consume entertaining content. Popular music was no longer the only option. A listener could tune in for alternative or classical sounds and tune out reigning popular trends.

---

190 Putnam, *Bowling Alone*, 216-245.
191 Ibid.

2. **The dawn of electronic technologies that allowed people to consume media in private**—Putnam recognized a change in the way Americans were participating in leisure entertainment. Prior to the television era, low-cost entertainment was primarily available in communal settings—baseball parks, dance halls, movie theaters. But, in the last half of the 1900s, television took leisure entertainment into our homes and allowed us to shut out the broader world.

Think about it this way: if you're tired, why get all dressed up to go when you can get a healthy dose of gossip from your friends, *The Real Housewives of Beverley Hills*, all from the comfort of your own bed?

The Real Housewives rose to fame a bit after Putnam's book, but a look at more recent data from the Pew Research Center seemingly supports Putnam's theories.

Let's start with a look at news readership.

Now, Putnam found in his research that "those who read the news are more engaged and knowledgeable about the world than those who only watch the news."[192] Further, those regular newspaper readers generally "belong to more organizations, participate more actively in clubs and civic associations, attend local meetings more frequently, vote more regularly, volunteer and work on community projects more often, and even visit with friends more frequently and trust their neighbors more."[193]

---

192 Ibid.
193 Ibid.

But, as Putnam observed in the early 2000s, newspaper circulation was already declining, a trend he attributed to the rise of television. People, he hypothesized, must be watching the news, not reading it. In reality, however, "Americans who watch the news on television are *more* likely to read the daily newspaper than are other Americans, not less likely. In the lingo of economics, TV news and the daily newspaper are complements, not substitutes."[194]

And, much to Putnam's dismay, engagement with the news on broadcast networks appeared to be falling as well. He found "while the average age of the audience for all prime-time programs was forty-two, the average age of the audience for nightly newscasts was fifty-seven."[195]

Putnam concluded then that interest in the news as a whole was declining generation-over-generation.

And when he looked at news media on the internet, he found that as usage of the internet expanded in the second half of the 1900s, usage of it to follow public affairs became relatively *less* important. In short, the newer media are mainly drawing on the steadily shrinking traditional audience for news, not expanding it.[196]

Finally, those who got their news primarily from the internet—unlike those who read the newspaper or watch the nightly news on television—were actually *less* likely than

194 Ibid.
195 Ibid.
196 Ibid.

their fellow citizens to be civically involved, a correlation that suggests the internet could be a factor for increasing isolation of American communities, but cannot be proven. It is entirely possible that those early internet adopters were simply more withdrawn from civic events to begin with.[197]

Today, we see that this trend has more-or-less held steady.

Circulation for American newspapers continues to fall. The estimated total US daily newspaper circulation (print and digital combined) in 2018 was 28.6 million for weekdays and 30.8 million for Sunday, down 8 percent and 9 percent, respectively, from the previous year.[198]

While there is some debate over whether or not these declines account (fully) for the digital reach of online outlets, one thing is clear. Time spent on digital news sites, a key metric of reader engagement, is falling. In the most recent Pew data, which looked at Q4 2018, the center found that among the top fifty US daily newspapers, based on circulation, average time on site per visit was only about 2.33 minutes, a drop of about 5 percent year-over-year.

In 2018, social media sites surpassed print newspapers as a news source for Americans. According to Pew, "one-in-five US adults say they often get news via social media, slightly higher than the share who often do so from print newspapers (16 percent)."[199]

197 Ibid.
198 Pew Research Center, "Newspapers Fact Sheet" July 9, 2019.
199 Shearer, "Social media outpaces print newspapers in the U.S. as a news source," December 10, 2018.

And Pew found fairly similar generational trends to Putnam in its latest analysis.

The report finds that age gaps have widened substantially, with those "65 and older five times as likely as 18- to 29-year-olds to often get news from TV. A large majority of those 65 and older (81 percent) get news from television often, as do about two-thirds (65 percent) of those 50 to 64. Far fewer young Americans are turning to television news, however—only 16 percent of those 18 to 29, and 36 percent of those 30 to 49 get news often from television."[200]

Among those aged 30 to 49, online news outlets are more popular. Among this group, about 42 percent frequently get their news from websites and news apps and 27 percent of 18- to 29-year-olds get their news from online news websites and apps, making it now the second most commonly used platform for news consumption among the young-American age group.[201]

But 18- to-29-year-olds are most likely to get their news from social media. Thirty six percent get news on social media most often, topping online news (27 percent), TV (16 percent), radio (13 percent), and print (2 percent). Younger Americans are also unique in that they don't rely on one platform in the way that the majority of their elders rely on TV. No more than half of those aged 18 to 29 and 30 to 49 get news often from any one news platform.[202]

---

200 Pew Research Center, "Newspapers Fact Sheet," July 9, 2019.
201 Ibid.
202 Ibid.

One more alarming stat to share: According to data from the Bureau of Labor Statistics' Occupational Employment Statistics, "37,900 people worked as reporters, editors, photographers, or film, and video editors in the newspaper industry in 2018. That is down 14 percent from 2015 and 47 percent from 2004."[203]

So, we have fewer people interested in the news itself, resulting in a decline of revenue for news media outlets, causing a reduction in the number of people employed as credible reporters, all while we're seeing a massive expansion in the amount of content we can consume and when we can consume it.

Looking back to Putnam's work, the proliferation of TV programming hit America at the exact moment that "general civic disengagement" was expanding. He found, "in a correlational sense...more television watching means less of virtually every form of civic participation and social involvement."[204]

These are the findings of a society with access to approximately forty channels on cable television.

Now, I ask you to imagine how this trend might accelerate in a world where most American consumers subscribe to three streaming services, each with hundreds and hundreds of shows and movies—tailored to an individual's interests—readily available for on-demand play.

So, considering that in Putnam's examination of American culture, the rise of choice in content and introduction of new

---

203 Ibid.
204 Putnam, *Bowling Alone*, 228.

forms of mass media—including television and the internet—coincided with an overall decline in national social connectivity, we can infer that as our content options have expanded, social connectivity has further deteriorated.

In an increasingly disconnected society, social media provides a way for users to encounter information that matters most to them to their own networks. However, exposure to news content and current events doesn't seem to be moving the needle for news engagement among social media users.

When Pew asked users what they enjoyed about getting the news on social media, Americans cited the convenience of the platforms. Twenty-one percent of Americans noted that social media is "very accessible," "it's available at the touch of a button," and "I don't have to go looking for it" as the leading benefit of reading news on social sites.[205] Speed and timeliness are cited as additional benefits of social media as a platform for news consumption.

As the Pew research found, "respondents also say they like the interpersonal element: 8 percent of social media news consumers say they enjoy interacting with others—whether through discussing the news, sharing news with friends and family, or seeing what others' opinions are."[206]

---

205 Shearer and Matsa, "News Use Across Social Media Platforms 2018," September 10, 2018.
206 Ibid.

But, disturbingly, a majority of Americans who consume news on social media, 57 percent, say they expect the news they see on social media to be largely inaccurate.[207]

The Pew report further noted, "among Republican social media news consumers, 72 percent say they expect the news they see there to be inaccurate, compared with 46 percent of Democrats and 52 percent of independents. And while 42 percent of those Democrats who get news on social media say it has helped their understanding of current events, fewer Republicans (24 percent) say the same. Even among those Americans who say they *prefer* to get news on social media over other platforms (such as print, TV or radio), a substantial portion (42 percent) express this skepticism."[208]

This data paints a pretty grim outlook for American trust in the news, and the general disengagement with news content would seem to suggest that we're likely trending toward further national civic detachment. But, I don't believe that all hope is lost.

I actually see great promise in the youngest set of social media users—the tweens.

A GENERATION OF COMPETITIVE CONTENT CREATORS

I spend a lot of time babysitting my younger cousins and every time these tweens have to explain to me a new trend

---

207 Ibid.
208 Barthel and Mitchell, "Americans' Attitudes About the News Media," May 10, 2017.

taking the internet by storm, I age approximately a hundred years in their minds.

I thought that I was an early adopter of social media, because I was a teen when Myspace was cool and I was heading to college while Facebook was still new and required a university email address to register. But, by today's standards, I am a very, very late adopter of social media.

For my cousins, YouTube and TikTok are absolute requirements in their social lives. In a pandemic-driven content ecosystem, TikTok is becoming a lot more mainstream. Celebrities are filming TikTok videos and posting them on highly followed social accounts (mostly Instagram) and, as a result, more and more people are downloading TikTok.

But I am getting ahead of myself. Do you know what TikTok is? I will explain.

TikTok is a video app, owned by a Chinese internet company, that enables users to easily create, edit, and share brief videos and share with the entire TikTok userbase. The goal is to generate viral content that other users will replicate.

And TikTok has—like many platforms before it—changed the game for content creation.

TikTok users can scroll through an infinite pool of content organized for discovery and, when they find a video that is particularly entertaining, they can pull the audio file and recreate it for themselves and seamlessly edit and share with the ecosystem.

My first exposure to the app was through the summer of 2019 phenomenon, "The Git Up." This western-inspired rap clip, lip sync, and dance video features a stiff-armed shuffle, "two-step," a bespoke dance move called a "cowboy boogie," and instructs the dancer to "grab your sweetheart and spin out wit' 'em." It's incredibly catchy.

The dance rose to popularity after one young user, @Harvey-Bass from the UK, posted his version of the dance recorded from his school's cafeteria. "I got suspended for this," his caption declares. It broke through the noise and went viral, globally.[209]

So, fast forward a bit to see me, my sister and our twelve-year-old cousin on a July 4th weekend at the shore—definitely following one too many glasses of wine for us over twenty-one-year-olds—strategically placing a cell phone on the steps to capture our video at the perfect height, adjusting the lighting in the hallway so we don't look washed out, and running through at least ten takes of the dance before determining that we had truly nailed the Git Up. Then, we hit share to a network of strangers on TikTok and anxiously awaited the "likes" our dance video would receive.

Shortly after The Git Up had its moment, the *New York Times* ran its first feature focused on these very young video influencers emerging as a result of YouTube and TikTok. The

---

209 tik tok senpai, "Harvey Bass the git up tik tok" YouTube, 0:18.

article dug into a video content development conference in California, called VidCon:

"If you can look past the silliness and status-seeking, many people at VidCon are hard at work...Many social media influencers are essentially one-person start-ups, and the best ones can spot trends, experiment relentlessly with new formats and platforms, build an authentic connection with an audience, pay close attention to their channel analytics, and figure out how to distinguish themselves in a crowded media environment—all while churning out a constant stream of new content."[210]

These young storytellers are learning, incredibly early on in their lives, how to capture mind share—an industry term referring to consumer awareness and popularity—and hold attention. And, in much the same way that the Kardashians have "Trojan horsed" a lot of important topical discussions into "what appears to be a vapid reality show," I believe that these young content creators battling for virality will have the upper hand in steering online conversation in the future, whether that be in media, politics, business, or entertainment.[211]

ENTERTAINMENT AND ADVOCACY

As I am writing this book, there is a worldwide movement for social equality and acknowledgement of systemic racism, and much of the organization of this movement has occurred

210 Roose, "Don't Scoff at Influencers. They're Taking Over the World," July 16, 2019.
211 Ryan, *Glitter Room,* Netflix, 2019.

over social media. Much of this movement has been mobilized by Gen Z.

Gen Z, born between 1995 and 2010, are true digital natives. They have grown up with the internet, social networks, and mobile computing. Access to sprawling sources of information is not only natural for them, but expected, and as a result they know how best to navigate the information in search of truth.

In this regard, it seems like Gen Z has found a way around the pitfalls of individualism that my millennial peers fell victim to. Their native connectivity and acceptance of online networking as an extension of physical interactions makes them more open to diverse perspectives than those of us who experienced life before the internet and social media took over.

Consider this digitally savvy generation in the context of the Black Lives Matter movement.

Black Lives Matter initially began in 2013 following the death of Trayvon Martin and the acquittal of George Zimmerman, the man who fatally shot him. The then movement gained further momentum with the deaths of Michael Brown and Eric Garner. In 2014, the social media hashtag #BlackLivesMatter peaked at 146,000 tweets.[212] But, in 2020, following the highly public, graphic death of George Floyd, who suffocated while a white police officer knelt on his throat, the

212 Andrews. "Tinder, TikTok and more: Online activists are finding creative new ways to say Black Lives Matter." *The Washington Post.* June 12, 2020.

Black Lives Matter movement re-surged with greater energy and advocacy than ever before.

As of May 28, 2020, Twitter reported that the #BlackLivesMatter hashtag had been used more than 8 million times.[213] Many of those mentions are driven by Gen Z's use of social media platforms to organize for action. They are rallying people for protest, promoting petitions for policy changes, and asking law enforcement to take substantive action.

Gen Z's radical inclusiveness manifests in their online and real-world interactions. According to McKinsey, Gen Z doesn't distinguish between the friends they have met online and those they know in the physical world. They use this extended personal network, made possible by technology, to bring together diverse voices and mobilize action around causes and interests they value most highly.[214]

Having grown up in an online environment, Gen Z is plugged into the internet at all times. They easily navigate the flood of content around Black Lives Matter and share the most relevant information on demonstrations, police activity, and local activist communities. They share incredibly practical information, like phone numbers for civil rights lawyers you can contact if arrested and instructions for what to do if you are exposed to tear gas.[215]

---

213 Ibid.
214 Francis and Hoefel, "'True Gen': Generation Z and its implications for companies," November 12, 2018.
215 Bellan, "Gen Z Leads The Black Lives Matter Movement," June 12, 2020.

Chelsea Miller, co-founder of Freedom March NYC, a newly formed youth-led organization that mobilizes non-violent protests to fight for Black youth issues, told a *Forbes* reporter that "we had to take control of the narrative because it's our story. It's our lives. We have a responsibility to tell it right for the future generations to come."[216]

I find it so interesting that Miller refers to this moment as a story and narrative that can be shaped. That term is, I believe, indicative of this generation's acknowledgement of the role of content in our culture and, inherent in that, the role every individual plays in shaping that content.

So, where my peers piloted the influence economy, Gen Z has realized its true potential, rejecting the performative reality we see day-in and day-out, and instead finding new ways to break through the noise and make their own perspectives heard.

In response to the anti-racist movement, Democratic leaders held a moment of silence at the Capitol, where they donned African stoles and knelt on the floor while cameras captured their demonstration. But Gen Z called them out. One viral Twitter posts from @assiahayth wrote, "Politicians are so performative like why are they kneeling when they could literally change the law???? Like bitch get up and perform your JOB."[217]

And that sentiment is not the rarity among Gen Z's protest engagement. These activists are logging into TikTok

---

216 Ibid.
217 J assia, Twitter post, June 8, 2020.

to share protest activity, posting confrontations with their own parents about race, and reflecting on their own experiences with race in America. Miller's co-founder, Nialah Edari, stated that she believes Gen Z is "interested in things that are cut simple, engaging, and easy to share," and as *Forbes* notes of their interview "a simple message is not an insincere one."[218]

218 Bellan, "Gen Z Leads The Black Lives Matter Movement," June 12, 2020.

TAKING BACK
THE POWER

Fame can be addictive.

Kim Kardashian West has admitted it herself.[219]

In an interview she and her husband, Kanye West, gave to *Vogue Arabia*, Kardashian shared—in response to a question from her husband about her opinion on her money and fame, "Money was always the goal but I was obsessed with fame, like embarrassingly obsessed."[220]

And our relationship with celebrities is just as addictive as their relationship to fame itself.

---

219 Alexandra Gouveia, "Kim Kardashian West Interviewed by Kanye West for Her First Vogue Arabia Cover," *Vogue Arabia*, August 26, 2019. https://en.vogue.me/fashion/kim-kardashian-west-kanye-west-vogue-arabia-cover/ (Accessed June 20,2020).

220 Ibid.

In his book, *Fame Junkies*, Jake Halpern observed:

"Since the early 1960s, the Gallup Organization has been conducting a poll about which man Americans most admire and compiling a list of the top twenty or so overall finishers. In 1963 that list included a number of political figures—Lyndon Johnson, Winston Churchill, Charles de Gaulle, and Martin Luther King Jr. among them—but not one entertainment celebrity, sports star, or media personality. By 2005 the list included six such people: Mel Gibson, Donald Trump, Bono, Michael Jordan, Arnold Schwarzenegger, and Rush Limbaugh."[221]

It is exactly this shift in where we place our admiration that captured my attention throughout working on this book.

For centuries, we have equated renown and fame with power, merit, and civic virtue. Regardless of the manner in which a celebrity achieved fame, there is a certain aspect of our psychology that recognizes the power that their position in the social stratosphere now awards them.

Today, being a celebrity equates to being powerful. Influential. And we, a society rooted in ideals of upward mobility, yearn for that status and obsess about those who have achieved it.

"The sad thing about [fame] is people that desperately need to become famous. It's like a drug...when you meet them they are desperate, desperate for it," remarked PR agent and "fame-maker" Max Clifford in an interview with *Psychology*

---

221 Jake Halpern, *Fame Junkies*, Kindle Cloud Reader, Location 94.

Today.[222] "It totally takes over [their lives]...They tend to isolate themselves from people that actually know them and possible care about them because they aren't there anymore. They then become surrounded by people who...say what the person wants to hear all the time. They become wrapped up in fame and get a totally jaundiced picture of life and reality."[223]

Well, lucky for those thirsting for fame and renown, technology has certainly made achieving fame more accessible than ever before.

EASY ACCESS FUELS ADDICTION

As a child, I was able to log onto our family computer and use a dial up connection to stream live radio out of Nome, Alaska so that I could follow the happenings of the Iditarod dog sled race (I was a big fan of the cartoon movie *Balto*).

Now, this was back when the internet was still a channel used to amplify our traditional media channels—in this case, Alaska Public Radio station KNOM. But from my small town in New Jersey, I was seamlessly plugged into a sledding tradition in Alaska with the click of a mouse.

I want you to recall with me these early days of the world-wide-web. When we looked to homepage sites like MSN and Yahoo to aggregate news from a variety of sources—vetted sources, like the *New York Times* and the *BBC*. These sites

---

222 Mark Griffiths, "Why We Seek the High of Stardom," March 24, 2014.
223 Ibid.

curated a holistic view into the news of the day and gave everyone everywhere a universal view into what would have traditionally been local news, because we were no longer limited by the constraints of physical publication and distribution.

News about the Iditarod wasn't exactly top-of-the-fold in Ho-Ho-Kus, New Jersey, but with a search run through my homepage, a brief software download, and a lot of buffering, I could listen in as the racers I had learned about reached checkpoints along the track from Anchorage to Nome.

But today, our experience is entirely different.

No one in their right mind would work as hard as I did to listen to radio updates. Everything we do today is powered by the entertainment industry, and much of it seamlessly delivered to our cell phones via social media updates.

Much of the expansion of this media has happened over the past decade. In fact, in 2005, the US Department of Labor cited an "explosion of programming" fueling job growth of 31 percent in the television industry.[224] And reality TV programming—a hugely profitable business model for the entertainment industry—drives a big portion of that expansion.

If our access to substantive celebrity news and programming is expanding, wouldn't that suggest that our addiction to celebrities is similarly expanding?

---

224 Jake Halpern, *Fame Junkies*, Kindle Cloud Reader, Location 171.

In his book, *Fame Junkies*, Jake Halpern observes that when discussing addictive substances, authorities recognize that the more available the addictive substance is, the greater the number of people who form addictive relationships with it.[225] So, per the same line of thinking, he suggests that our relationship with fame is likely similarly self-perpetuating. The more visible and accessible our famous celebrities, the more we, the viewers, want to watch.

It builds a self-fulfilling supply and demand issue. We crave the content, and so our content universe expands, which requires more democratic celebrities to program for us, which makes achieving fame more accessible, which makes more of us thirst for fame. And, repeat.

Now, add to this supply and demand cycle a cultural inclination to ascribe credibility, power, and influence to those who have achieved renown and you have the equation that has enabled such rapid influence economy growth and expansion.

So, what do we do about it?

REDUCING THE IMPACT OF INFLUENCERS
I mentioned at the start of this project that I wanted to understand why it was I watched so much reality programming, and I believe that I got to the heart of it. I am a human being and, being human, I crave interpersonal interaction.

---

225 Jake Halpern, *Fame Junkies,* Kindle Cloud Reader, Location 259.

But my lifestyle—defined by long hours at work, limited attachment to my local community, and general enjoyment of time spent alone on my couch in sweats—makes it a bit harder for me to get the person-to-person community feeling that we, as humans, crave. So, instead, I switch on the E! network and get a healthy dose of gossip from someone else's life to round out my day.

You can feel sad for me. It's fine. But at least now I recognize that I'm doing it.

For many of us, especially those living in bigger cities, it's likely that we know more about highly residual celebrities like the Kardashians than we do about the people living and working next door to us. Our loose connections to each other and limited engagement with our communities have opened the door to an expanded ecosystem of surreal-realities in which we can escape and, ultimately, connect.

Bonnie Fuller, the chief editorial director for American Media Inc., the tabloid conglomerate that publishes the *Star*, the *National Enquirer*, and the *Globe*, observes, "What is going on is that that we all have fewer people in common... When you're in high school, or at a small college, you know everybody's business and you can follow their romantic goings-on and discuss them with your friends. But when you grow up and you're out in the work world, you don't have that. So, celebrities give us a whole world of people in common—people to gossip about at work over the water cooler or at a dinner party." [226]

---

226 Jake Halpern, *Fame Junkies,* Kindle Cloud Reader, Location 2283

And maybe we should lean into that gossipy nature to find the solution.

Stick with me.

A psychologist, Robin Dunbar, shared that "the term gossip itself did not originally have that [negative] meaning. It meant simply the activity that one engaged in with one's 'god-sibs,' one's peer group equivalent of godparents: in other words, those with whom one was especially close."[227]

So, instead of letting our relationships with these celebrities (who we have already determined have opted into this lifestyle and are actively seeking our gossip to fuel their own economic interests) allow us to further isolate from our direct community, let's lean into our pop cultural obsessions to bring us closer together.

We, as people, want to be entertained. We crave gossip. We attach to narratives. And, more than anything, we want to connect with each other. And while we maintain a bias for entertainment, the influencer economy will continue to expand.

This doesn't have to be a bad thing. We just need to redirect our understanding of influencers and celebrities toward their original economic purpose: entertainment.

Let's take the wealth of content influencers create on a daily basis and start up new conversations that might bring back some of the community we've let erode over the past decades.

---

227 Jake Halpern, *Fame Junkies,* Kindle Cloud Reader, Page 145

Start talking about reality TV like you would a trip to the theater, if any of us could afford (or would even be allowed) to go to the theater anymore. Recognize it as an art form. A commentary on our culture.

Laugh about the crazy table-flipping housewife from whatever show was being broadcast to the nation the night before. Settle in to watch two star-crossed aspiring influencers on *The Bachelor* proudly declare that they are in love one day after meeting, because these people live for our entertainment.

I believe their influence can only be as powerful as we, society, allow it to become. So, talk about how what you watched was artfully designed to give you something to talk about. And in doing so, begin to distance yourself from manufactured relationships with those "just like us" and instead, foster a deeper connection with others who truly are *just like us*.

Because the more we talk about the surreal nature of the influence economy, the wiser we'll be to its effects.

APPENDIX

INTRODUCTION

- Bank, Dylan and Daniel DiMauro. *Get Me Roger Stone.* VOD. Directed by: Dylan Bank and Daniel DiMauro. Worldwide: Netflix, 2019).

- Bueno, Antionette, "Kim Kardashian Shares Picks of Khloe Going to Jail for Throwback Thursday," *ET Online,* March 10 2016, https://www.etonline.com/news/184233_kim_kardashian_throwback_thursday_is_when_khloe_went_to_jail, Accessed July 3, 2020.

- Chesney, Brandon (@deadpriate). "He finally got his meeting with Kim!" Twitter post. May 30, 2018. https://twitter.com/deadpirate/status/1001983053001117696?s=20.

- Forbes, Kim Kardashian West Profile. Last updated July 10, 2019. https://www.forbes.com/profile/kim-kardashian-west/#-1c5a580d41d6.

- Fox, Emily Jane. "Keeping up with the Kushners: With Jared back on top, Kim Kardashian heads to the White House." *Vanity Fair*, May 30, 2018.

- Friedman, Megan and Erica Gonzales. "Here's How Much Every Member of the Kardashian–Jenner Family Is Worth." Harper's Bazaar. April 26, 2020. https://www.harpersbazaar.com/celebrity/latest/a22117965/kardashian-family-net-worth/.

- Fry, Naiomi. "Kim Kardashian Meeting Donald Trump in the Oval Office Is a Nightmare We Can't Wake Up From." *The New Yorker*, May 31, 2018.

- Hardwood, Erika. "Kim Kardashian says Donald Trump was 'Compassionate' in Oval Office Meeting." *Vanity Fair*, June 8, 2018.

- Kardashian West, Kim (@kimkardashian). "Happy birthday Alice Marie Johnson. Today was for You." Instagram photo, May 30, 2018.

- *Keeping Up With the Kardashians*. Season 3, Episode 1. "Free Khloe." Produced by Ryan Seacrest Productions, Featuring Kim Kardashian West, Kris Jenner, Khloe Kardashian, Kourtney Kardashian, Kylie Jenner, Kendall Jenner, Rob Kardashian, Caitlyn Jenner, Malika Haqq, Shawn Chapman Holley, aired on March 8, 2009, on E!.

- Pfeiffer, Dan (@danpfeiffer). "A photo of a reality TV star with no discernible talent, but famous for being famous and a Kardashian." May 30, 2018 https://twitter.com/danpfeiffer/status/1001962329884512258?s=20.

- Piazza, Jo. *Celebrity, Inc. How Famous People Make Money.* (New York: Open Road Integrated Media, 2011) 101-103.

- Ryan, Katherine. *Glitter Room.* VOD. Directed by: Linda Mendoza. Worldwide: Netflix, 2019.

- Schnieder McClain, Amanda. *Keeping up the Kardashian Brand: Celebrity, Materialism and Sexuality.* (Plymouth, U.K.: Lexington Books, 2014), 10.

- The New York Daily News (@NYDailyNews). "An overrated reality TV star met with Kim Kardashian https://nydn.us/2L8RZoB. Here's a look at Thursday's front..." Twitter post. May 30, 2018. https://twitter.com/NYDailyNews/status/1001990216549322752?s=20 .

- *The New York Post.* Front Page, May 31, 2018.

- Trump, Donald (@realDonaldTrump). "Great meeting with @KimKardashian today, talked about prison reform and sentencing." Twitter post. May 30, 2018. https://twitter.com/realDonaldTrump/status/1001961235838103552?s=20.

- Yardley, William. "Bill Loud, the Father of TV's 'An American Family,' is Dead at 97." *The New York Times*, July 27, 2018. https://www.nytimes.com/2018/07/27/obituaries/bill-loud-dead-american-family.html?login=smartlock&auth=login-smartlock (accessed June 12, 2020).

CHAPTER 1

- Baxter-Wright, Dusty, "How did Kim Kardashian Actually Get Famous? A Timeline of Her Career," *Cosmopolitan*, September 27, 2017. https://www.cosmopolitan.com/uk/entertainment/a12464842/who-is-kim-kardashian/ (accessed July 5, 2020).

- Currid-Halkett, Elizabeth. *Starstruck: The Business of Celebrity*. New York. Farrar, Straus and Giroux. 2011. Kindle Cloud Reader. Location 431.

- Harding, Amanda. "Why Is Kim Kardashian West Famous?" *Showbiz Cheat Sheet*. March 5, 2019. https://www.cheatsheet.com/entertainment/why-is-kim-kardashian-west-famous.html/ (Accessed June 14, 2020).

- Lawrence, Rebecca. "Vicky Pattison joins Lauren Goodger in sending support to Khloe Kardashian amid cheating scandal... despite having never met her." *Daily Mail*. April 12, 2018. https://www.dailymail.co.uk/tvshowbiz/article-5606821/Vicky-Pattison-joins-Lauren-Goodger-sending-support-Khloe-Kardashian-amid-cheating-scandal.html (accessed June 14, 2020).

- Lorenz, Taylor. "Welcome to the Era of Branded Engagements." *The Atlantic*, June 20, 2019. https://www.theatlantic.com/technology/archive/2019/06/was-viral-proposal-staged/592141/ (accessed June 14, 2020).

- Sanders, Sam. "'The New Celebrity': The Rise of Influencers— And How They Changed Advertising." September 10, 2019. In *It's Been A Minute*. Produced by Anjuli Sastry. Podcast, MP3 audio, https://www.npr.org/transcripts/759127302 (accessed June 14, 2020).

CHAPTER 2

- Currid-Halkett, Elizabeth. *Starstruck: The Business of Celebrity*. New York. Farrar, Straus and Giroux. 2011. Kindle Cloud Reader.

- Frier, Sarah. *No Filter: The Inside Story of Instagram*. New York. Simon & Schuster. 2020.

- USC Price. "Starstruck: The Business of Celebrity—USC Literary Luncheon." May 12, 2011, video, 51:49, https://www.youtube.com/watch?v=PQi8UXZV-o4.

CHAPTER 3

- Braudy, Leo. *The Frenzy of Renown: Fame and Its History.* (New York: Vintage Books, a division of Random House, Inc., *1986, 1997)* Heffernan Virginia, "The Elusive Price—and Prize—of Fame on the Internet." *Wired.* August 20, 2019. (accessed on June 14, 2010).

- Currid-Halkett, Elizabeth. *Starstruck: The Business of Celebrity*. New York. Farrar, Straus and Giroux. 2011. Kindle Cloud Reader.

- Frier, Sarah. *No Filter: The Inside Story of Instagram*. New York. Simon & Schuster. 2020.

- Scheiner McClain, Amanda. *Keeping Up the Kardashian Brand: Celebrity, Materialism, and Sexuality.* (New York: Lexington Books, 2014).

- USC Price. "Starstruck: The Business of Celebrity—USC Literary Luncheon." May 12, 2011, video, 51:49.

- Waters, Mark. dir. *Mean Girls.* 2004; Hollywood, CA: Paramount Pictures, 2004.

CHAPTER 4
- Currid-Halkett, Elizabeth. *Starstruck: The Business of Celebrity.* New York. Farrar, Straus and Giroux. 2011. Kindle Cloud Reader.

- de Tocqueville, Alexis. *Democracy in America. Edited by Richard D. Heffner,* (London: Signet Classics 2001), 5.

- Dickinson, Emily. "Fame is a fickle food." *The Poems of Emily Dickinson,* Edited by R. W. Franklin (Cambridge, Harvard University Press, 1999.) https://www.poetryfoundation.org/poems/52134/fame-is-a-fickle-food-1702 (Accessed on June 14, 2020).

- Grabb, Edward, Douglas Baer, and James Curtis. "The Origins of American Individualism: Reconsidering the Historical Evidence." *The Canadian Journal of Sociology / Cahiers Canadiens De Sociologie* 24, no. 4 (1999): 511-33. Accessed June 14, 2020.

- Jefferson, Thomas. "First Inaugural Address." March 4, 1801, https://avalon.law.yale.edu/19th_century/jefinau1.asp (accessed June 14, 2020).

- *Love and Hip Hop: New York.* Season 5, Episode 2. "You're Cancelled." directed by produced by Toby Barraud, featuring

Cisco Rosado and Diamond Strawberry, aired December 22, 2014, on VH1.

- Memedroid. https://www.memedroid.com/memes/detail/2635843/A-lot-of-you-have-asked-about-my-skin-care-routine (Accessed June 14, 2020).

- Romano, Aja. "Why we can't stop fighting about cancel culture." Vox. *December 30, 2019.* https://www.vox.com/culture/2019/12/30/20879720/what-is-cancel-culture-explained-history-debate (accessed June 14, 2020).

- Scheiner McClain, Amanda. *Keeping Up the Kardashian Brand: Celebrity, Materialism, and Sexuality.* (New York: Lexington Books, 2014).

CHAPTER 5

- Adams, James Truslow. *The Epic of America.* (New York: Little Brown & Company, 1931).

- Ahrens, Lynn. "Fireworks." *School House Rock.* Performed by Grady Tate. 1977. http://www.schoolhouserock.tv/Fireworks.html (Accessed June 14, 2020).

- *Keeping Up With the Kardashians.* Season 10, Episode 9. "Lip Service." Produced by Joshua Hardnen and Jacob Lane. Featuring Kylie Jenner, Kim Kardashian West, Kris Jenner, Khloe Kardashian, Kourtney Kardashian, Kendall Jenner. Aired May 10, 2015 on E!

- King Jr., Martin Luther. "Letter from a Birmingham Jail." UPenn: Center for African Studies. https://www.africa.upenn. edu/Articles_Gen/Letter_Birmingham.html (Accessed June 14, 2020).

- Lorenz, Taylor. "The Instagram Aesthetic is Over." *The Atlantic. April 23, 2019.* https://www.theatlantic.com/technology/archive/2019/04/influencers-are-abandoning-instagram-look/587803/ (Accessed June 14, 2020).

- Robehmed, Natalie. "At 21, Kylie Jenner Becomes the Youngest Self-Made Billionaire Ever." *Forbes.* March 5, 2019. (Accessed June 14, 2020).

- Sanders, Sam. "'The New Celebrity': The Rise of Influencers— And How They Changed Advertising." September 10, 2019. In *It's Been A Minute.* Produced by Anjuli Sastry. Podcast, MP3.

CHAPTER 6

- Cialdini, Robert B., *Influence: The Psychology of Persuasion.* (New York: Collins Business, 2007). 274.

- Comscore. "2016 U.S. Cross-Platform Future in Focus." March 30, 2016. https://www.comscore.com/Insights/Presentations-and-Whitepapers/2016/2016-US-Cross-Platform-Future-in-Focus. (Accessed June 14, 2020).

- Edgecliffe-Johnson, Andrew. "Murdoch predicts the demise of classified ads." *Financial Times.* November 24, 2005. https://www.ft.com/content/6b49e6ba-5d11-11da-a749-0000779e2340 (accessed June 14, 2020).

- Gold, Howard R. "Who Killed Time Inc.?" *Columbia Journalism Review.* February 1, 2018. https://www.cjr.org/business_of_news/time-inc-meredith.php (Accessed June 14, 20202).

- Goldsmith, Belinda. "Porn passed over as Web users become social." *Reuters.* September 16, 2008. https://www.reuters.com/article/us-internet-book-life/porn-passed-over-as-web-users-become-social-author-idUSSP31943720080916?pageNumber=1 (Accessed June 14, 2020).

- Huey, John. Twitter Post. January 31, 2018. 11:13 PM https://twitter.com/johnwhuey/status/958916249802694657.

- Jenner, Kylie. Twitter Post, May 29, 2020, 11:52 AM. https://twitter.com/KylieJenner/status/1266396922752843779.

- Jenner, Kylie. Twitter Post, May 20, 2020, 11:52 AM. https://twitter.com/KylieJenner/status/1266397099349864448.

- Malle, Chloe. "How Billion-Dollar 'Unicorns' Are Changing the Beauty Industry." *Vogue.* July 22, 2020. https://www.vogue.com/article/billion-dollar-unicorns-vogue-august-2019-issue (Accessed June 14, 2020).

- Martin, Demetri. "Trendspotting: Social Networking." *The Daily Show with Jon Stewart*, February 15, 2006. http://www.cc.com/video-clips/dxrlhk/the-daily-show-with-jon-stewart-trendspotting---social-networking (Accessed June 14, 2020).

- Mejia, Zemina. "How Kylie Jenner turned her $29 lipstick business into a $420 million empire in 18 months." CNBC. September 14, 2017. https://www.cnbc.com/2017/09/14/how-ky-

lie-jenner-turned-kylie-cosmetics-into-a-420-million-empire.
html (accessed June 14, 2020).

- Omnicore. "Instagram by the Numbers: Stats, Demographics
  & Fun Facts." February 10, 2020 https://www.omnicoreagency.
  com/instagram-statistics/ (Accessed June 14, 2020).

- Peterson-Withorn, Chase and Madeline Berg. "Inside Kylie
  Jenner's Web of Lies and Why She's No Longer a Billionaire."
  Forbes. May 29, 2020. Updated June 1, 2020. https://www.forbes.
  com/sites/chasewithorn/2020/05/29/inside-kylie-jennerss-web-
  of-lies-and-why-shes-no-longer-a-billionaire/#42860d3225f7
  (accessed June 14, 2020).

- Pew Research Center. "Newspapers Fact Sheet." July 9, 2019.
  https://www.journalism.org/fact-sheet/newspapers/ (Accessed
  June 14, 2020).

- Robehmed, Natalie, "At 21, Kylie Jenner Becomes the Youngest
  Self-Made Billionaire Ever." Forbes. March 5, 2019. (Accessed
  June 14, 2020).

- Sanders, Sam. "'The New Celebrity': The Rise of Influencers—
  And How They Changed Advertising." September 10, 2019. In
  It's Been A Minute. Produced by Anjuli Sastry. Podcast, MP3
  audio, https://www.npr.org/transcripts/759127302 (accessed
  June 14, 2020).

- Schonfeld, Eric. "Zuckerberg: We Are Building a Web Where
  the Default Is Social." TechCrunch. https://techcrunch.
  com/2010/04/21/zuckerbergs-buildin-web-default-social/#:~:-
  text=Zuckerberg%3A%20%22We%20Are%20Building%20

A,The%20Default%20Is%20Social%22%20%7C%20TechCrunch. April 21, 2010 (accessed on June 14, 2020).

- Statista. "Number of monthly active Facebook users worldwide as of 1st quarter 2020 (in millions)." April 30, 2020, https://www.statista.com/statistics/264810/number-of-monthly-active-facebook-users-worldwide/#:~:text=How%20many%20users%20does%20Facebook,network%20ever%20to%20do%20so (Accessed June 14, 2020).

- Stone, Mike and Michael Flahretty. "Icahn buying up Time Warner shares: sources." *Reuters* January 11, 2016. https://www.reuters.com/article/us-timewarner-icahn-idUSKCN0UQ03A20160112. (Accessed June 14, 2020).

- Strugatz, Rachel. "Kylie Jenner's Kylie Cosmetics on Its Way to Becoming $1B Brand." *Women's Wear Daily*. August 9, 2017. https://wwd.com/beauty-industry-news/beauty-features/kylie-jenner-cosmetics-to-become-billion-dollar-brand-10959016/ (Accessed June 14, 2020).

- Waters, Mark. dir. *Mean Girls.* 2004; Hollywood, CA: Paramount Pictures, 2004.

- Zorthian, Julia. "Kylie Jenner's Cosmetics Brand Is on Track to Become a $1 Billion Company." *Fortune*. August 10, 2017. https://fortune.com/2017/08/10/kylie-jenner-kylie-cosmetics-worth/ (Accessed June 14, 2020).

CHAPTER 7

- Baer, Susan. "Jacqueline Kennedy helped define the terms history uses about JFK The Mystique of Camelot." *The Baltimore Sun,* May 27, 1995. https://www.baltimoresun.com/news/bs-xpm-1995-05-27-1995147124-story.html (Accessed June 14, 2020).

- Deery, June. *Reality TV.* (Cambridge, U.K. Polity Press, 2015).

- McAfee, Tierney and Liz McNeil. "How Jackie Kennedy Invented Camelot Just One Week after JFK's Assassination." *People Magazine.* November 22, 2017. https://people.com/politics/jackie-kennedy-invented-camelot-jfk-assassination/. (Accessed on June 14, 2020).

- Ostergaard, Shelby. "Jackie Kennedy Onassis: An Icon for the Ages." CommonLit. 2018 https://www.commonlit.org/en/texts/jackie-kennedy-onassis-an-icon-for-the-ages (Accessed on June 14, 2020).

- Poniewozik, James. "The Real Donald Trump Is a Character on TV." *New York Times Opinion. September 6, 2019.* https://www.nytimes.com/2019/09/06/opinion/sunday/trump-reality-tv.html (Accessed on June 14, 2020).

- Shakespeare, William. *The Merchant of Venice.* 1600.

- Sydney, Hugh. "Camelot." *The Kennedy Assassination Chronicles,* Fall 1995. http://www.jfklancer.com/pdf/Camelot.pdf.

- USC Price. "Starstruck: The Business of Celebrity—USC Literary Luncheon." May 12, 2011, video, 51:49.

- White, Theodore H. "For President Kennedy: An Epilogue." *LIFE.* December 6, 1963. https://www.jfklibrary.org/asset-viewer/archives/THWPP/059/THWPP-059-009 Accessed on June 14, 2020.

CHAPTER 8

- Andrews, Travis M. "Tinder, TikTok and more: Online activists are finding creative new ways to say Black Lives Matter." *The Washington Post.* June 12, 2020. https://www.washingtonpost.com/technology/2020/06/12/tiktok-tinder-twitter-bts-black-lives-matter/ (Accessed on June 14, 2020).

- Assia. Twitter post, June 8, 2020, 2:53 PM. https://twitter.com/assiahayth/status/1270066312124010496.

- Barthel, Michael and Amy Mitchell. "Americans' Attitudes About the News Media Deeply Divided Along Partisan Lines." *Pew Research Center,* May 10, 2017. https://www.journalism.org/2017/05/10/americans-attitudes-about-the-news-media-deeply-divided-along-partisan-lines/ (Accessed June 14, 2020).

- Bellan, Rebecca. "Gen Z Leads the Black Lives Matter Movement, on and off Social Media." *Forbes.* June 12, 2020. https://www.forbes.com/sites/rebeccabellan/2020/06/12/gen-z-leads-the-black-lives-matter-movement-on-and-off-social-media/#-f09e90119a88 (Accessed June 14, 2020).

- Francis, Tracey and Fernanda Hoefel. "'True Gen': Generation Z and its implications for companies." McKinsey. November 12, 2018. https://www.mckinsey.com/industries/consumer-packaged-goods/our-insights/true-gen-generation-z-and-its-implications-for-companies#. (Accessed June 14, 2020).

• Goldsmith, Belinda. "Porn passed over as Web users become social." *Reuters*. September 16, 2008. https://www.reuters.com/article/us-internet-book-life/porn-passed-over-as-web-users-become-social-author-idUSSP31943720080916?pageNumber=1 (Accessed June 14, 2020).

• Pew Research Center. "Newspapers Fact Sheet." July 9, 2019 https://www.journalism.org/fact-sheet/newspapers/ (Accessed June 14, 2020).

• Putnam, Richard. *Bowling Alone: The Collapse and Revival of American Community*, (New York: Simon and Schuester, 2000).

• Roose, Kevin. "Don't Scoff at Influencers. They're Taking Over the World." *The New York Times*. July 16, 2019. https://www.nytimes.com/2019/07/16/technology/vidcon-social-media-influencers.html (Accessed on June 14, 2020).

• Ryan, Katherine. *Glitter Room*. VOD. Directed by: Linda Mendoza. Worldwide: Netflix, 2019.

• Shearer, Elisa. "Social media outpaces print newspapers in the U.S. as a news source." *Pew Research Center*, December 10, 2018. https://www.pewresearch.org/fact-tank/2018/12/10/social-media-outpaces-print-newspapers-in-the-u-s-as-a-news-source/ (accessed June 14, 2020).

• Shearer, Elisa and Katerina Eva Matsa. "News Use Across Social Media Platforms 2018." *Pew Research Center*, September 10, 2018 https://www.journalism.org/2018/09/10/news-use-across-social-media-platforms-2018/#most-social-media-news-consumers-are-concerned-about-inaccuracy-but-many-still-see-benefits (Accessed June 14, 2020).

- Tik tok senpai. "Harvey Bass the git up tik tok." YouTube. 0:18. https://www.youtube.com/watch?v=MHBGLt_2ri4 (Accessed June 14, 2020).

CHAPTER 9

- Gouveia, Alexandra. "Kim Kardashian West Interviewed by Kanye West for Her First Vogue Arabia Cover," Vogue Arabia, August 26, 2019. https://en.vogue.me/fashion/kim-kardashian-west-kanye-west-vogue-arabia-cover/ (Accessed June 20,2020).

- Griffiths, Mark. "Why We Seek the High of Stardom." *Psychology Today*, March 24, 2014. https://www.psychologytoday.com/us/blog/in-excess/201403/why-we-seek-the-high-stardom#:~:-text=In%20an%20article%20in%20the,or%20situation%5D%20will%20trigger%20cravings.(Accessed June 20, 2020).

- Halpern, Jake. *Fame Junkies: The Hidden Truths Behind America's Favorite Addiction.* (Boston: Houghton Mifflin Company, 2007). Kindle Cloud Reader

ACKNOWLEDGEMENTS

First and foremost, I want to thank my family for their support throughout the process of completing this book. My mom, dad, and sisters—Aly and Lee—were my primary sounding boards, the original beta readers and provided the most supporting, honest, thought provoking feedback I could have imagined. Getting to talk about pop culture, reality TV, and celebrity gossip with the four of you over these past months has been an absolute blast, and I can't thank you enough for all of your help.

To Tim Hughes, who let me spend the first two weeks of our life together in Tulsa, Oklahoma frantically writing and editing in our mostly-empty apartment as I finished this book: thank you for your support and for cooking dinner. I love you.

As I was working on this book, I had the opportunity to interview a number of people in the and entertainment industries—some of whom I've worked with for years, some of whom graciously lent their time to a stranger, and all of whom asked not to be directly named in this book. To those of you who shared your insights, perspectives, and healthy doses of gossip: thank you.

To Professor Patrick Deneen: thank you for taking time out of your schedule to reconnect with a former student trying to uphold a commitment to a life of learning. Your insights and direction were an enormous help as I worked my way through an ocean of research.

To those of you who provided feedback and direction throughout this process—including Jillian Conrad, Brenna Dougherty, Matthew Portanova, Andrea Portanova, Patty Portanova, Kevin Norton, Katie Norton, Elizabeth Norton, Alexandra Rossetti, Katie Zanone, and Donna Zanone—I cannot tell you how helpful your feedback has been and I hope you see a bit of yourselves in the end result.

Finally, to the team at New Degree Press, especially Eric Koester, Brian Bies, Jordan Waterwash, Cynthia Tucker, Michelle Felich, Gjorgji Pejkovski, Josip Perić, and Alexander Svistakov an enormous THANK YOU for your direction, support, feedback, and guidance throughout the process of finalizing this book. I can genuinely say, I don't think I could have done it without you.

Made in the USA
Monee, IL
10 August 2020